The Vanishing of Subhash Bose

The Vanishing of Subhash Bose:
The Mystery Unlocked

BY

Rajesh Talwar

KALPAZ

First Published, 2020
Published by

Kalpaz Publications
C-30, Satyawati Nagar,
Delhi – 110052
Ph.: 011-47034999, 9811692060
www.kalpazpublications.com
E-mail: kalpaz@hotmail.com

Printed at: G. Print Process, Delhi

Cataloging in Publication Data—DK
Courtesy: D.K. Agencies (P) Ltd. <docinfo@dkagencies.com>
Talwar, Rajesh, author.
The vanishing of Subhash Bose : the mystery unlocked / by Rajesh Talwar.
pages cm
ISBN 9789353242404
1. Bose, Subhas Chandra, 1897-1945—Death and burial. 2. Nationalists—India—Biography. 3. Governmental investigations—India. 4. India—Politics and government—20th century. I. Title.

LCC DS481.B6T35 2020 | DDC 954.035092 23

Contents

The White Rats and the Brown Mice

A few white rats get into a house full of thousands of brown mice. The white rats being bigger and more powerful take charge of the house and command the timid mice to do their bidding, which they do for many years. Over time however some mice rebel and refuse to do the rats bidding anymore. More and more of the brown mice are pulled to the movement known as 'non-cooperation'. Meanwhile a few hundred mice escape from the house, team up with other mice in the neighbourhood and start to give the house a good shake from the outside. Inside the house, the white rats confer hurriedly. The provisions inside the house have mostly already been looted and little remains. They are increasingly disturbed by the mice inside the house who are not offering any cooperation and the mice outside who are shaking the house. They decide to leave. Only the white rats themselves know which mice troubled them more. Once they leave the brown mice inside the house take charge, take full credit for getting rid of the white rats, and assume control of the house. The brown mice who worked so hard from the outside are completely ignored.

Synopsis

Netaji Bose, wholed the Indian National Army to wage battles against the British, allegedly died in an air crash in Taipei, Taiwan soon after the Second World War came to an end. Did he really die in the air crash or was it a fabrication? This question was considered by three inquiry commissions, the last of which came to the clear conclusion that there was in fact no air crash. Each report is carefully dissected by the author, a trained lawyer and UN official.

If Bose did not in fact die in the air crash, where did he go, what happened to him, and when, where and how did he meet his end?Why did Prime Minister Nehru keep Bose-related files away from the first committee that conducted an enquiry? Why did India's first prime minister order that surveillance be carried out on the Bose family for decades? Why did Prime Minister Morarji Desai speak of new evidence that challenged the conclusions of the first two inquiries that Bose had died in an air crash? Why did Desai subsequently fall silent? This book provides explanations on all the important questions that have plagued Indian minds for decades. The mystery behind the springing tiger's disappearance is finally unlocked.

If Gandhi's non-violent struggle represented the feminine spirit of 'ahimsa' Bose and the INA's struggle represented Indian manhood in its fullest flowering. In freedom struggles across the world, some of those who fought the hardest are subsequently ignored. If we apply the necessary corrective to the history of Indian independence, the author argues, we will change India's view of itself and its place in the world, past, present and future.

Preface

As a writer I've sometimes thought about writing a thriller on the lines of one of the fast paced American novels I grew up reading. These suspenseful stories are often formulaic in terms of the plot. Typically the hero is a spy or agent, but for various convoluted reasons – the need for to protect the high and mighty – the Central Intelligence Agency (CIA), who happens to be his immediate employer disowns him. As a consequence, he is frequently on the run, escaping assassins and dodging bullets from both sides: those who are clearly his enemies, but also those who were supposed to be his friends and protectors but have turned against him.

I never wrote that book but the life and times of Subhash Chandra Bose can be likened to one such thriller. If I were to make a film on the subject, instead of the blockbuster Hollywood film 'Crouching Tiger, Hidden Dragon' I would choose 'Springing Tiger, Crouching Dragons,' for here the tiger is springing, not crouching. It is the 'dragons' who are both hidden and crouching.

Who is this springing tiger? It is in fact the epithet for Subhash used by Hugh Toye[1] the English author of a book on Netaji and the Indian National Army (INA). This particular term was used for Bose because a springing tiger was the insignia on the INA uniform. If the 'springing tiger' represents Netaji, as any lover of this freedom fighter will already know, who then are the 'crouching dragons' in this book's title?

The dragon has always been a symbol of great power, which begs the question: why are these powerful dragons crouching? Could it be that the dragons are crouching for they know that the truth if revealed will neutralise their power. They have adopted a crouching stance to prevent that from happening. More pointedly perhaps who are the dragons?

Certainly, in relation to Bose, the Allied Forces in World War 2 were 'dragons'. Subhash represented an enemy for them, having joined forces with the Axis powers, notably Japan. These were however the known enemies in our hero's story, but as is the case with the American thrillers I allude to, were there also others who were supposed to be his friends and protectors but who betrayed him? Were there important people who were leading the Indian freedom movement, fighting for the same cause as it were, although on different fronts, who should have been loyal to Bose, a fellow freedom fighter and erstwhile member of the Congress, but in fact abandoned him as soon as the reins of power fell into their grasp?

Was Subhash Bose not 'the spy who came in from the cold,'[2] the title of a John Le Carre classic, but rather a patriot who was left out in the cold? The allegation that he was left out in the cold and the contributions he and the INA made for the country downplayed is an allegation that is difficult to refute.

The only Bose in this book is Subhash Chandra Bose sometimes referred to as Subhash Bose or simply Subhash. To avoid confusion, especially for the foreign reader all the other Boses in that large family are referred to as Basu, a reasonable substitute. Suresh Chandra, Netaji's elder brother, a member of the first committee that probed the air crash and author of the 'Dissentient Report is referred tomostly as Suresh Basu but sometimes as Suresh Babu.

Subhash came from the traditional large Indian family of a bygone era. Cricket had not yet taken the Indian nation by storm, but Bose's father had produced a full cricket team in the house (with even a couple of players to spare in case someone suffered an injury or disqualification). Bose had thirteen siblings. From eldest downwards he was number nine in the list, which explains why one of his nephews was old enough to assist him in his escape from Calcutta where he was under constant British surveillance but nonetheless managed to give them the slip. It was Sarat Basu's son Sisir Kumar Basu, Bose's nephew, who acted as his driver and transported him from Kolkatta to Gomoh from where he boarded a train to Peshawar.[3]

A few words now about the structure and chapterisation of this book. Chapter 1 is titled 'Gandhi, Nehru and Bose.' For many years Subhash Bose had given his heart and soul to the Congress Party and in fact had been elected President of the party twice, the first time unanimously. In 1939 following a victory over Gandhi's nominee, Sitaramayaa, ironically enough, despite being elected President, Bose had to leave the party. There were major disagreements over the strategy to attain freedom between Gandhi and himself. It seems appropriate at the outset of the book to give some background of 'the springing tiger' and some sense of his position in the Congress, his relationship with Gandhi and how he compared with other stalwarts such as Nehru and Sardar Patel.

Chapter 2 of the book is titled 'Nehru and his Strange Surveillance'. It is now a matter of public record that the government led by Jawaharlal Nehru, India's first prime minister spied on Bose for nearly twenty years.[4] Leading news papers, as well as the prominent weekly magazine *India Today*, have discussed this issue at length. The facts themselves appear to be beyond dispute. Each and every letter that was sent to Bose's family after his alleged death was first intercepted by the Intelligence Bureau. It was carefully read, and copies were made before being sent on its onward journey. Was this merely oversight on the part of the Indian government who merely extended the surveillance originally imposed by the British? Was this surveillance ordered by Prime Minister Nehru, and if so, was it motivated by the purest and highest motives, all in the interests of the nation?

Chapter 3 is titled is 'The First Committee: Shah Nawaz versus Suresh Babu.' At the time the story of Netaji's death in an airplane crash came out in the papers many Indians across the country but more especially in West Bengal did not believe the story put out. Even Gandhi's initial reaction was to dismiss the story as pure rubbish. The controversy continued to brew even after India became independent. Post-independence Prime Minister Nehru fiercely resisted the demand for an enquiry, but eventually bowed to public pressure and constituted a three-member committee on 3 December1955 to examine the issue. This Committee came to a majority decision that Netaji had indeed died in the crash but there was a lone but powerful voice of dissent – that of the third member, Suresh Basu, who was also Subhash Bose's elder brother.

Both Western historians and Indian historians – the latter possibly seeking to curry favour with the ruling Congress – have been overly dismissive of Suresh Basu's dissenting opinion. Yes, the language may be flowery, and Basu is prone to use the extra-long sentence, but there is nothing that a good editor could not have easily fixed in a few hours. Leave aside editorial services, Suresh Basu, poor fellow, was even denied access to many documents available with the other two committee members once it was clear that he would not toe their line! The historian Leonard Gordon points out that there is repetition in his report, but is that such a serious flaw?[5] In any event it is not as frequent and annoying to a reader as has been made out.[6] Gordon appears to have completely misread and misunderstood Suresh Basu's reasons for dissenting; in this regard he has been extraordinarily unfair to Bose's elder brother. On a dispassionate reading of Suresh Basu's '*Dissentient Report,*' although certain prejudices do surface, in general an impartial reader cannot fail to be impressed with the passion and logic with which the elder sibling presents his arguments.

In this chapter I have sometimes paraphrased but more often used the original wording used by Suresh Basuto provide the reader with a sense of authenticity. I did not wish to be too much of an interpreter, leaving the reader to make up his own mind on what Suresh Babu and the witnesses he quotes might have meant. This chapter focuses on the fallacies and defects in the majority opinion as articulated by Bose's elder brother.

Why is there greater focus in this chapter on the Suresh Basu's 'Dissentient Report' than on the main Justice Shah Nawaz Report? Surveillance carried out of the Bose family for over two decades' under Nehru's direction screams out for a re-evaluation of the Shah Nawaz Committee majority opinion as well as Suresh Babu's courageous Dissentient Report. Poor Suresh Basu never realised that he too was being spied upon even *as he sat on the Committee.* Nehru did not grant him an exemption from surveillance. In the event that there was a 'Deep Throat' somewhere in India or abroad who sought to notify Suresh Basu of important information regarding his brother's disappearance, the Intelligence Bureau and Pandit Nehru would have their hands on such information before it reached him, if it ever did. It would after all be the government's decision whether or not to forward any such communication on to Suresh Basu! It is a damning indictment of the first decades of Indian democracy that the entire Bose family was being watched. Can you imagine? An important member of the Shah Nawaz Committee appointed by Nehru, a real brother of Subhash Bose no less, Suresh Basu was under surveillance (together with the others in the Bose family) *even as the Committee of which he was a member continued his deliberations*. The Shah Nawaz Committee was appointed in April 1956 and concluded its interviews within four months in July, 1956 with extraordinary speed, unheard of in a government committee. Even as it investigated and deliberated, a member of the Committee was being watched by the intelligence arm of the government together with the rest of the Bose family. One wonders at the sheer brazenness and shamelessness of the powers-that-be. It is also clear that journalists of that time were either clueless about the spying by the government or strangely silent.

The following chapter, Chapter 4 is titled 'A Tale of Two Commissions'. Partly as a result of Suresh Chandra Basu's dissenting opinion the controversy did not die down. Fourteen years later, on 11 July, 1970, Nehru's daughter, Indira Gandhi appointeda one man Commission under the leadership of Justice G D Khosla. Judge Khosla supported the opinion of the earlier

Committee and came to the conclusion that Netaji had died in the crash. Around the same time that he wrote his report, he unfortunately also published a hagiography of the then Prime Minister Indira Gandhi.[7] It started to look as if the judge might not have been free from bias or prejudice while writing his report. As a consequence the public was, once again, left unsatisfied. There is an adage that justice must not only be done, but it must be *seen* to be done.

Thus we had a situation where the first Committee that considered the matter was riven by conflict with the third dissenting Committee member accusing the other two of withholding documents from him. The independence of the second body, the Justice Khosla Commission was also called into question. Two reports down, and the public was not satisfied that the truth had been unearthed or even that a bona fide attempt had been made to uncover it.

Rumours continued to fester, and fifteen years later in1999 once again a Commission was set up. The sitting Supreme Court Chief Justice was called upon to provide advice on who could be the most suitable retired judge to handle the enquiry. He may have deliberately suggested an erstwhile judge of the Apex court who happened to be a Bengali. Surprise, surprise, the Justice Mukherjee Commission, as it was called, eventually went against the findings of the previous two bodies and concluded that it was clear that Subhash Bose had NOT died in the crash and further that the ashes at the Renkoji Temple in Japan did NOT belong to the venerable leader.

The next few chapters in the book continue to focus on the Justice Mukherjee Commission Report and discuss how it came to the conclusions referred to above. This special focus on the Mukherjee report is logical for several reasons. It is the most recent body to consider the matter of Netaji's 'disappearance' and therefore had the benefit of reviewing earlier reports. The judge was appointed by a non-Congress government and cannot be accused of being a Congress *chamcha*, an allegation that could have been levelled against Justice GD Khosla. Allegations can also be levelled at Shah Nawaz Khan who chaired the first Committee. While it is true that Khan was a public hero and fought for the Indian National Army, at the same time, he was a Minister in the Congress Government, and was someone whom Barrister Nehru, not yet Prime Minister, had defended at the Red Fort trials. Such allegations cannot however be levelled against Justice Mukherjee.

Justice Krishna Iyer wrote in one of his famous judgements: 'Legalese and logomacy (sic) have the genius of injecting mystique into the meaning of words, thereby alienating the laity from the rule of law.' In places where Justice Mukherjee's writing is dense I have tried to simplify the language without losing sight of the original meaning.

Chapter 5 of the book is titled 'Stonewalling Justice Mukherjee.'It sets out the background against which the Commission was set up, outlines the mandate and resources available to it and discusses the procedure followed by it before arriving at its conclusions. A truth finding body, Justice Mukherjee faced numerous obstacles. In this chapter we see his valiant but unsuccessful efforts at unearthing the truth from government files. The Mukherjee Commission tried its best to get hold of certain files that could reasonably have been presumed to exist on the basis of statements made by Prime Minister Morarji Desai on the floor of the house but it came up against a resistant bureaucracy that kept stonewalling its efforts. The Judge has no choice but to come to the conclusion that the government was being deliberately evasive and was definitely hiding something.

After appointing him though, for reasons that are still shrouded in mystery, the Bhartiya Janata Party (BJP) led government changed its mind about cooperating with the commission. Justice Mukherjee comes across as someone who could not be pressured, for at this stage it appears that neither the Congress nor the ruling BJP wished to have a verdict that concluded that Netaji had not died in an air crash.

Chapter 6 is titled 'The Crouching Dragons.' The expression 'crouching' brings up a visual of a creature tensed up at the prospect of the truth behind Netaji's disappearance being revealed. The 'dragons' represent powerful forces that will make all efforts in keep a lid on things. Nehru, some argue, had a vested interest in preventing the truth from coming out. A common argument advanced is that he may have felt that his position as prime minister endangered. After all if Nehru was not willing to play second fiddle to Sardar Patel, (which has been well documented[8]) he would certainly not have been willing to be second to Bose. Was Nehru a dragon? If this was indeed the case, it can be reasonably inferred that the Congress Party too had a vested interest in preventing the truth from coming out. Was the so-called Grand Old Party of India also a dragon? At the time the Mukherjee Commission was constituted it was not however the Congress but the opposition National Democratic Alliance (NDA) government that was in power under Prime Minister Atal Bihari Vajpayee.[9] Some years previously as an opposition leader Atal Bihari had been actively protesting the Congress government's inaction on this issue. What had happened to make this confident orator change his stance? Why had he (and his government) also started to behave like dragons?

What about the Indian communists, who should have been sympathetic to Bose, since he himself was known to be left leaning? After all the Communist Party of India (Marxist) was the ruling party in West Bengal for decades, even as the Congress ruled the Centre. Why was it so quiet? Why did it not take up the issue? Why did they not de-classify Netaji related documents held in the State government archive that was within its prerogative? Was this simply insensitivity or was it too part of the coalition of crouching dragons? Did Nehru know something about Bose's disappearance that Sardar Patel did not? Patel was the Home Minister. Would it have been possible for Nehru to have known things that Patel was not privy to? Or was it possible that Patel actually agreed with Nehru that some disclosures were best withheld – in the greater public good. This chapter considers this and other questions.

Chapter 7 is titled 'Testing the Ashes'. With new DNA technology, lots of old unsolved murders have been solved the world over. These days there are commercial organisations that will even track down your ancestry based on a DNA sample. The Mukherjee Commission spent time and effort trying to see if the new DNA technology could somehow determine whether or not the ashes kept at the Renkoji Temple in Japan belonged to Subhash Bose. The great irony here is that there *has* been DNA testing of the remains of Gumnami Baba, a swami claimed by some to be Netaji in disguise, but there has been no testing of the ashes at RenkojiTemple!It is true that a test of burned bones *might not* eventually settle the issue but *at least an attempt should have been made.* The chapter examines what this technology can achieve, what it cannot, and the struggles of the Mukherjee Commission – the only one of the three enquiries that could potentially have used DNA technology to assist it in its investigations.

The next chapter, chapter 8, is titled 'A Final Breakthrough at Taipei'. One of the most obvious leads that anyone investigating Netaji's disappearance should have followed was to simply ask the Taiwanese government if there had indeed been an air crash at the relevant location at the relevant date, and if so, could it provide details. The First Committee never visited Taiwan; permission for doing so was withheld by Nehru. Judge Khosla, appointed by Indira Gandhi, did visit Taiwan but never asked this simple question. It is astonishing that this was not done by the Judge. It is as if the police are sent to investigate a car crash, they know that there is an eye-witness to the accident, but they file their report without bothering to question that witness. The Taiwanese government and its people are the biggest witness to what happened, even though they were not in power then – and they were not even asked! Justice Mukherjee does not make the mistake made by his predecessors and he does achieve a break through!

Chapter 9 is titled 'Fanciful Disappearance and Death Theories'. Various explanations were provided by Bose-lovers, some seemingly logical and others out landish and even over-the-top on what happened to Netaji. The Mukherjee Commission considered the more prominent of these theories and gave its opinion on them. At least three of the theories have Netaji appearing in a saintly *avatar*. This would suggest that people *wish* to believe that Netaji became a *sadhu* or holy man. Chapter 9 discusses these theories of Netaji's disappearance, alleged reappearance and some other unsubstantiated submissions made by various conspiracy theorists. In his report, Justice Mukherjee did not find favour with any of these theories. Finally, in this chapter we discuss the conclusions and comments of the Commission. The Mukherjee Commission came to the conclusion, as mentioned earlier, that there was no reason to suppose that Netaji died in the crash, or even that a crash took place. It was all, it would seem, a game of mirrors. As stated previously Judge Mukherjee also came to the conclusion that the ashes at Renkoji Temple did not belong to Netaji.

If Netaji did not die in an air crash, because, quite simply the crash never took place, what happened to him. He could not have stayed on in Japan without being arrested, so the question arises: where did he go?

Chapter 10 examines the 'Netaji-went-to-Russia' theory, which surfaced soon after the alleged air crash. This chapter examines Netaji's options, which were not so many. He could not have gone to China which had been occupied by Japan. He could not have sought refuge in any of the countries that had supported the Allied war effort. Had Netaji ever expressed his wish to go to Russia? Why was Russia the most likely option? If he went to Russia why did the millions of Indians who loved him never hear of him or from him again?

It would not make sense to complete this book without giving my own view of the questions that have surfaced. I endeavour to do provide my opinion in the second last chapter of the book,

Chapter 11, which is titled 'What Nehru Knew.' I accept Justice Mukherjee's clear conclusion in his report that it is evident that Netaji did not die in the air crash. What happened subsequently is something we will never know with certainty, because no matter how many new files are resurrected from the dead, none of them are likely to contain information that will conclusively settle the questions. The 'dragons' have had time enough to clean up all the evidence.

Does this mean that we should give up? No. There *is* a way. Just as there are two ways to describe the truth, there are two ways to ascertain the truth. Many years ago in school my Sanskrit teacher was discussing Meghdoot (Cloud Wanderer) that immortal classic penned by the poet Kalidas. He told us how the poet described Shakuntala's beauty not directly but through the journey of a drop of water falling from a tree on to our heroine. That drop of water is a witness to her beauty. Who is the drop of water in this case? Who is the witness in the case of Bose? It is none other than his erstwhile colleague in the Congress Party, Jawaharlal Nehru. The reader and I both know that there were things that Nehru knew, which never came out, and will never come out in the future. From a reading of Nehru's personality and a study of his actions we can make an intelligent guess as to what happened to Nehru, where did he go and when did he die. I endeavour to answer all these questions in this chapter of the book. No spoilers here.

The mystery surrounding Bose's disappearance is now unlocked but there still remains a last chapter without which the book would be incomplete. This is Chapter 12 titled 'The Real Crime against Bose' and it discusses the crimes committed against Bose by Nehru, by successive Indian governments, and by historians in their account of India's freedom struggle.

Why this book? A question may be raised as to the need to publish this book. After all there are already numerous writings and even books on the subject of Netaji's disappearance. Additionally, there are conclusions and reports issued by a

Committee and two Commissions, with some (though not all) of the material available in the public domain. There are writings by Harvard professor Sugata Basu which support the government's stance that Netaji died in an air crash. This is also the position of Columbia University historian Leonard A Gordan.[10] On the other hand we have a Commission of Inquiry chaired by a former judge of the Indian Supreme Court who has sifted through new evidence that emerged following his visit to Taiwan which makes him conclude in his report, without any equivocation, that the air crash was a fabrication. There was no air crash – and therefore there is no question of Bose having died in it. This book will clear the air some what.

It doesn't really matter that the State Government files are now declassified because the possibility of finding something of value there, in the context of Netaji's disappearance are minimal. It is also more or less certain that what was truly of value has already been destroyed insofar as the files in the custody of the government are concerned. Netaji was under surveillance for years before his eventual disappearance and it is likely that most of the files deal with his India period before he escaped under the very nose of the British, or with a period that was much before his eventual disappearance. They may therefore shed little light on what happened to him.

The great thinker Renan writes in a famous essay that part of nationhood involves a forgetting of the past. Historically, there was at one time fierce fighting between the north and south of France, but subsequently all of that was forgotten, and France was one. Renan writes eloquently on how in his view: 'Forgetting, I would even say historical error, is an essential factor in the creation of a nation, and it is for this reason that the progress of historical studies often poses a threat to nationality.'[11] Similar reasoning resonated with Gandhi who thought that the brutal treatment meted out to Hindus by Islamic invaders such as Mahmud of Ghazni and Mohammad Ghori were best forgotten? In other words, to use the old English idiom, 'Let bygones be by gones.'

Gandhi and Renan were both right that forgetting is something good for a nation, but that logic does not apply in the context of what happened to Subhash Bose. As a nation we should remember Bose and the thousands of Indian National Army (INA) fighters who sacrificed their careers, families and even gave their lives for the freedom of the country. The history which is taught in schools across India only fleetingly dwell on how thousands of INA soldiers died fighting the British in Burma and the North East, if they do even that.[12] There is no contradiction in school children taking pride in the 'ahimsa' preached by Gandhi as well as the not-so-nonviolent fighting spirit of many Indian heroes. We do not have to hark back to Hindu or Muslim heroes of the pre-British past to take pride in Indian manhood. We have equally poignant tales in the more recent past of idealistic and matchless heroism in which Hindus and Muslims fought shoulder to shoulder. It is not my intention to denigrate Nehru in this book, but I do wish for India to properly honour Netaji for himself and as the representative of thousands of diehard patriots in the INA who suffered, sacrificed and died fighting for Indian independence.[13]

The material that follows has the potential to touch a dangerous nerve among the Indian political fraternity. Publishers are known the world over for their cowardice. Indian publishers are no exception and wouldnot wish to antagonise one of the most powerful families in the country. Even a relatively harmless book, a biography of Sonia Gandhi by the French writer Javier Moro was not available in bookstores till recently.[14] Even now, the Nehru-Gandhi family may be currently out of power, but they can conceivably make a comeback in the next parliamentary elections if the present government fails to deliver.

Historians in India from the right or the left, even as they oppose colonialism have often viewed Subhash Bose and the INA thorough that very same colonial lens. We, the people of India have the power to change the way the history of our struggle for independence from the British has been written till now. If we exercise that morally right choice, we will change India's view of itself, and its place in the world, past, present and future.

RT, Kabul
26 January 2020

Chapter - 1

Gandhi, Nehru and Bose

Do you want the fragrance of the full-blown rose? If so you must accept the thorns. Do you want the splendour of the smiling dawn? If so, you must live through the dark hours of the night. Do you want the joy of liberty and the solace of freedom? If so, you must pay the price. And the price of liberty is suffering and sacrifice.

Subhash Chandra Bose, *Bombay, 31.12.1931*

The Fight For the Congress Presidency

The adage that 'power corrupts' is a recognition of human frailty – even if it is somewhat doubtful that absolute power corrupts absolutely, for who in the world has absolute power and what is really meant by 'absolute power' or for that matter 'absolute corruption'? It could have been said rather, more accurately, though less dramatically, that power corrupts and more power often corrupts yet more. Despite the simplicity of his hermitic attire and living conditions, Gandhi too enjoyed power and the trappings of power after his own fashion. In the political sphere possibly the most shocking exhibition of the dictator hiding within the saint came to light when he overruled by Gandhian diktat the democratic election of Subhash Chandra Bose as Congress Party President.

Even Sunil Khilani, social historian and great admirer of the Mahatma, writes about how Gandhi subverted the democratic idea on very many occasions. 'For the duration of Gandhi's dominance, from 1920 until the early 1940's,' Khilnani writes, 'Gandhi preferred not to be a formal member of the Working Committee, yet he used it repeatedly to push through decisions that contradicted the wishes of party members. Most conspicuous was his removal of Subhash Chandra Bose from the elected office of Party President in 1939. He goes on to elaborate how Gandhi did establish a culture of dialogue and within the Indian National Congress but his fierce disciplinary regimes – fasts, silences and penances – gave him a grip on the party that relied at once on coercion and seduction.Khilnani writes:'*These were the immensely effective techniques of an eccentric parent, but they were not designed to nourish commitment to democratic institutions.*'[15]

As regards Bose's election Gandhi had in fact nominated someone else to be the candidate for Party President that year, and suggested that he be elected unopposed. Bose had not fallen in line with the saint's wish and decided to contest the election, which he won hands down. On 29 January, 1939 Bose was elected Congress Party President. Despite this victory, he could not properly savour its taste. Gandhi was extremely unhappy and declared: 'Sitaramayya's defeat is my defeat.'[16] Two swords cannot be placed within a single scabbard, as the Persian saying goes. Bose was compelled to leave the party. Possibly two diametrically opposed strategies for independence could not coexist within a single party. Even so was this not hypocrisy on the part of the Mahatma? If he didn't want anyone else but the person he nominated to be President of the party, why suggest the charade of an election?

Netaji was forced to resign because despite winning the Presidency of the party in a fair and open election, he became a President without a Working Committee. Gandhi would not accept his proposal that a composite Working Committee be formed with him and Sardar Patel nominating an equal number of candidates. Rudrangshu Mukerjee writes on how 'Gandhi emerges from this episode at his worst: petty and given to machinations, the archetypal Tammy Hall politician, his moral posturing not with standing.'[17]

What were Gandhi's misgivings? At one level he differed from Subhash's view that conditions in India were ripe for an ultimatum to the British and at another 'some what shadowy level was the presence of GD Birla' who disapproved of left leaning views.[18]

Thousands of Bose fans were immensely disappointed, even furious, at Bose having been outmanoeuvred by Gandhi and forced to resign in this manner. In Calcutta during an All India Congress Committee (AICC) meet the crowd turned angry when the news of Subhash's resignation spread. In fact Subhash had to personally escort many Congress leaders to ensure their safety. The great Bengali poet, Rabindranath Tagore expressed solidarity with his attitude and hailed him a true leader of India.[19] Subhash wrote to his wife Emilie to say: 'I have not lost anything by resigning. As a matter of fact I have become more popular now.'[20] In the next letter to her, he noted, 'India is a strange land where people are loved not because they have power but because they give up power. For instance at Lahore I had a warmer reception this time than when I went last year as Congress President.'[21]

Differing World Views

It could be argued that Bose had a view different world view from Gandhi's proclaimed non-violent approach, and so despite his popularity they could not have co-existed in the same institution. At the same time, it is saddening how over the years, the primacy of Gandhi in the struggle for Indian independence notwithstanding, Bose's contributions have been neglected. A little later in this book we will discuss unsubstantiated rumours that Nehru allowed Bose to die in a Soviet prison.[22] Be that as it may, there can be little doubt that part of the reason why Bose has become a shadowy figure on the margins of Indian history, instead of receiving his just due as being one of the major architects of Indian independence is owing to the fact that Gandhi's protégé Nehru, who became prime minister of the new India allowed this to happen.[23] Bose was no supporter of fascism, much less of Nazism but he supported the Germans and the Japanese in the World War because from his perspective it was the British who were the Nazis of India.

Giants of The Indian Freedom Movement

A century ago, the Dalit leader BR Ambedkar wryly noted how 'quite recently a new 'ism' had come on the Indian horizon. It is called Gandhism.' He adds that '(i) t is true that very recently Mr Gandhi has denied that there is such a thing as Gandhism. This denial is nothing more than the usual modesty that Mr Gandhi wears so well. It does not disprove the existence of Gandhism.'[24] In fact in a letter to Subhash Chandra Bose dated 30 March, 1939, the Mahatma himself uses the expression 'Gandhiites' though, typical of the man's careful modesty, he puts within parenthesises 'to use that wrong expression.'[25]

Bose's charisma was indisputable and legendary. Elected Congress Party president on two occasions, on the second occasion too he won the election hands down against Gandhi's nominated candidate. This fact alone testifies to his charisma and popularity. Nehru on the other hand could become Prime Minister only because he was the Mahatma's protégé. Even after Bose had left the Congress, Nehru could not garner much support. Had the Mahatma not placed his metaphorical hand over Nehru's slender shoulders in a real time contest with Patel, the Kashmir Pandit would not have survived.

All this is not mere speculation or conjecture but a matter of historical record. With Bose out of the picture, despite the Mahatma's clear support for Nehru, had there been a contest there is little doubt that Sardar Patel (who subsequently became Home Minister) would have been elected President of the party and would have been the first Prime Minister of India. Out of 15, 12 Congress Pradesh Committee's the only body with the power to nominate and elect the President of the Party nominated Sardar Patel.[26] Not a *single* Congress Committee nominated Nehru, but at the end of the day that did not matter. He was the Mahatma's blue eyed boy. Gandhi acted like the feudal lord he pretended he wasn't and 'advised' Patel to withdraw his candidature. He asked Acharya Kripalani to find a proposer and seconder for Nehru's candidacy.

The historian Rajmohan Gandhi records how 'as soon as Nehru had been formally proposed,' pursuant to the Mahatma's instructions Kripalani 'handed Patel a fresh piece of paper with the latter's withdrawal written out on it. Vallabhbhai was pulling out,Kripalani's draft said 'so that Nehru could be elected unopposed.'[27]

I mention the above episode only to show that had Bose been alive and present in India, post-independence, even outside the Congress, he would have given Nehru a run for his money for the top job in the country. Nehru knew somewhere that he could not compete with Bose on the popularity front.

To many in India – especially the post-independence generation – this might seem a false or exaggerated estimate, but they forget that they have grown up in an India that has been subjected to the Nehru family image-building exercise for decades. Nehru appears to them to be a giant – but much of that impression is due to billions of rupees spent in an image building exercise by Congress or government funds. The presence of rampant political *chamachagiri* in newly independent India also helped.

Post-independence Subhash Bose was largely ignored. Sisir Bose wrote bitterly to Emile, Bose's wife about how Subhash's role in the freedom movement was side-lined and downplayed. 'If you were in India today,' he wrote, 'you would get the feeling that in India's struggle two persons mattered – (Mahatma) Gandhi and (Jawaharlal) Nehru. The rest were just extras.'[28]

In a BBC interview, the Dalit leader Dr BR Ambedkar claimed to have known Gandhi better than others. Before others, Ambedkar alleged, the Mahatma exhibited only his famed fake politeness (shamelessly emulated by his followers, the so-called Gandhians, till this very day, some would say). 'In his meetings with me,' Dr Ambedkar said, 'his fangs came out.'[29]

In Subhash Chandra Bose's case, we see no 'fangs' but there does appears to have been acrimony on and off as is clear from the following excerpt from the Mahatma's letters. On 3 January,

1930 Gandhi wrote to Netaji from the Sabarmati Ashram a letter the opening paragraph of which is worth reproducing.

Dear Subhash Babu[30]

You are becoming more and more of an enigma to me. I want you to live up to the certificate that Deshbandhu once gave me for you. He pictured you to me as a young man of brilliant parts, singleness of purpose, great determination and above pettiness. Your conduct in Calcutta therefore grieved me, but I reconciled myself to its strangeness. But in Lahore you became inscrutable and I smelt petty jealousy. I do not mind stubborn opposition. I personally thrive on it, and learn more from opponents than from friends. I therefore always welcome sincere and intelligent opposition. But in Lahore you became an obstructionist. In connection with the Bengal dispute, in your writings to the Press you were offensive and the discourteous, impatient walk-out nearly broke my heart....

The Other Side of The Gandhi-bose Equation

Despite their not inconsiderable differences, it would appear that Gandhi and Bose enjoyed mutual respect. It was Subhash who coined the expression 'Father of the Nation' with reference to Gandhi. It is also significant, moving and to Subhash Bose's great credit that it was first used by him to symbolise Gandhi's contribution to the cause of Indian freedom, not when he was within the Congress fold but *much after there had been a clear parting of ways*. Bose's Indian National Army (INA) had already been formed. Clearly as far as Gandhi was concerned, Bose held little rancour or bitterness in his heart, or did not at any rate permit ideology to cloud his views of the saint and his contributions to the cause of India's freedom. After all Sardar Patel's objections to his candidature for the Presidency the first time round had been overruled by Gandhi, and he *had* consequently become Congress Party President.

There is an uncorroborated but plausible story in journalist Anuj Dhar's book in which a Congressman recalls Gandhi lamenting to him at the time the post-Partition riots broke out in India that he wished so very much that at that troubled moment in India's history 'his other son' was there. Who, asked the Congressman of Gandhi, was this 'other son'? 'Subhash,' was the Mahatma'sresponse. Nehru himself was overly dismissive of Gandhi's efforts to bring about a measure of peace through fasting and touring and said as much to his English friends.[31]He therefore refused to join the Mahatma in a fast, but even had he done so, possibly the add-on effect would have been inconsequential. The Muslim perception of Sardar Patel's secular credentials and bias towards the Hindus, even if ill-founded, might have affected the Sardar's ability to do much. In contrast, Bose's secularism was never in doubt and given his charismatic appeal across the nation, he could possibly have done much to stem the tide of violence and blood-letting at least in the State of West Bengal.

The Bias of Historians

The historian Mridula Mukherjee suggests that Bose was naïve enough to believe that fascism and communism had important things in common, not believing them to be 'polar opposites' as Nehru did.[32] We have the benefit of history (of what happened in communist regimes the world over from the killing fields of Cambodia to the gulags of the Soviet Union) to know that this idea of polar opposites was a myth. Subhash was right in his assessment even then in those early years of that great socialist political experiment. Historians both Indian and Western allege that Subhash was a man with a dictatorial mind-set and he wished to be 'The Leader.' And yet these very same historians when commissioned to write the history of the Congress choose to gloss over the Emergency and the authoritarianism of Nehru's daughter, Indira Gandhi. Arun Shourie writes in a book about the dominance of leftist historians in India;[33] this is only partially true. It would be more accurate to say that 'free' India has witnessed the joint dominance of both the leftist as well as the Congress-controlled historians. This is not in any way to condone the recent attempts by some right wing elements to re-write Indian history after their own fashion.

The Two Men – At Face Value

Jawaharlal Nehru was an extraordinarily good looking man. Beauty is said to rest in the eye of the beholder, on a dispassionate assessment Nehru could be said to be the more handsome of the two. Bose however was taller by a few inches; Nehru could have been said to be just falling short of being short. Subhash was bigger sized and had a broader frame as compared with Nehru, (who once stood on a stair to be shoulder to shoulder in a photo op with Lord Mountbatten, so that the two were on level). Both men were losing their hair.

Human beings get swayed by aesthetics while judging a person. In Greek history there is even a case where judges acquitted a woman accused of murdering her husband based only on her extraordinary beauty. So too there will be hundreds of thousands of people who will simply not believe that Nehru could ever have abandoned Bose. On Subhash Bose's part despite all his differences and subsequent bitterness with Nehru, he never ever forgot that they were soldiers in a common cause. He named one of the INA regiments after Mahatma Gandhi and he even named another one the 'Nehru Regiment'.

Unlike Gandhi, both Nehru and Bose eschewed simplicity, preferring the grand gesture. When Nehru became prime minister once he upbraided Lady Mountbatten for having arrived late for a meeting at his house. She explained that she was stuck in a traffic jam caused by the passage of the Prime Minister's (his, Nehru's) cavalcade.[34] Bose too did not look away from the symbolism of the occasional grand gesture. Suresh Babu recalls how, 'it was unique in the annals of the Congress when in 1928 he arranged a mile long procession for the President, Pandit Motilal Nehru on his arrival in Calcutta and led his volunteers on horseback as General Officer Commanding, in military formation through the streets of Calcutta.'[35] None of the other leaders would have fitted this role. Gandhi of course was above all this, and although he had previously served in the British army, he was now in any case a pacifist.[36] Nehru was too soft-hearted and romantic, and although a stylish dresser, his sartorial taste did not extend to the military uniform. It would also, perhaps, have seemed too 'royalist' to have the son leading the procession commemorating the father's appointment. Patel was too bulky and moreover was given to wearing the *khadi kurta* and *dhoti*, flowing Indian attire that was not suitable for such an occasion.

Ten years later at the Fifty-first Congress at Haripuara in 1938 Bose's political coronation was no less impressive. Hugh Toye writes: 'Proudly, in a Presidential car drawn by fifty-one bullocks through fifty-one gates of honour, he acknowledged nationalist India's fervent acclaim, not simply cheers for the new President, the new symbolic leader of the national struggle, but the fullness of hearts proud for his youth, his burning enthusiasm, his humanity and his new harmony with Gandhi.'[37]

Nehru and The Distortions in Indian History

Nehru's own papers are voluminous and have found pride of place in the Nehru Memorial Museum and the library at Teen Murti established in 1964 after Nehru's death. There are hundreds of thousands of documents, far greater than the number of documents concerning Subhash Chandra Bose, for the simple reason that Nehru became prime minister of India and remained so from 1947 up until 1963, a year or so after the Chinese debacle.

As regards pre-Independence history though, Bose could clearly have given Nehru a run for his money both in terms of quantity and interesting material. Yes, Nehru was involved closely together with Gandhi in dealing with Lord Mountbatten and helping India become a free country, but then Bose, on the other hand was raising an army, in record time, across different countries in South East Asia. The INA was also fighting battles, even if they were not being won!

The thousands of papers that have now been declassified (and the process continues) should have been released decades earlier. Just as there were repositories for Mahatma Gandhi's papers and Nehru's papers, so too should there have been a repository, possibly a large museum in central Delhi and Calcutta where the Bose papers should have been kept. They should have been microfilmed and historians given access to them to do research. The Bose papers would have shed light not only on the Indian National Army's struggle but on developments across the world, more specifically in Asia, in the context of the Second World War.

Nehru allegedly wept when he heard that Bose had died in an air crash. Sentimental Nehru was in charge of a trust that managed to send money to Bose's wife and daughter and money was paid to them till his death[38]. On the other hand there was no outreach to provide a pension to the brave soldiers of the INA who were settled in different parts of South East Asia. Further, Nehru refused to allow the Indian National Army to enter the regular Indian Army that came into existence post-independence. Even the contributions of INA soldiers in different parts of the world were never recognized, let alone providing them with an honorary citizenship. Nehru did nothing to stop the image building exercise that the Congress was crunching up on his behalf, but he made sure that even Bose's portrait did not adorn the Central Halls of Parliament. Today we know that the British left behind thousands of Bose-related documents that could and should have formed part of Indian historical research.

Was Nehru was a true lover of history? It is questionable, since he accepted the erasure of a large part of the history of the Indian freedom struggle. Perhaps history itself will someday judge the matter. Clearly he had read widely, but many scholars would be dismissive of his magnum opus 'Glimpses of World History' as essentially lightweight despite its impressive thickness without much original insight. He devoted large sections of that book to China, for he admired the Chinese and the achievements of their civilisation greatly and imagined that China and India were *bhai bhai* till Mao Zedong broke that illusion and Nehru's heart in the process. We now know that he ignored and succeeded in downplaying the role of the Indian National Army in India's independence. What is even more shocking is that thousands of Bose related papers were kept hidden in government archives gathering dust and mould following his clear instructions! It cannot be otherwise; there was no question but that he knew of this huge treasure trove of documents.

If someone were to create a mythology of the freedom movement on the lines of the great Indian classic, the Mahabharat, from the vantage point and view of the Congress mythology the heroic Pandavas were represented by Gandhi, Nehru and others, Bose would be considered to be the Karan of the Mahabharat, for had he not partnered with the evil fascists: Hitler, Mussolini and those of their ilk?

Yet on the other hand there will be those who will say, with possibly a greater degree of truth, that he was the one true Pandava, who saw and said clearly that the enemy of my enemy is my friend. In this reading of the Hindu epic it would be the British and their allies that represented Duryodhana and the Kauravs with whom Gandhi, Nehru and so many others had thrown in their lot. Subhash was the only true Pandav standing ready to battle the rest of the world if need be for the freedom of his motherland!

How should the history of the Indian freedom movement be written? Was Gandhi all-important or should we trust the purported remarks of British Prime Minister Clement Attlee, that it was Bose's efforts that really led the British to leave India. To neglect the role of Gandhi and the Congress would be an insult to Bose himself, for he knew better than to divide the struggle. For many in the Congress, Bose was a lost cause, a renegade, but Bose himself saw in the Indian National Army (INA) and the Gandhi led Congress efforts a common cause. In the INA there was not only a Rani of Jhansi regiment, a unique female force given the times but there was additionally a Nehru Brigade and a Gandhi Brigade[39].

For any true patriot, there ought to be no question of a choice really. One group was waging the war from within; the other was waging it from without. The two efforts represented the yin and yang of the struggle: feminine resilience combined with masculine fortitude. Even within India there were no such sharp divisions as the filmmaker Sagari Chhabra observes in her searing account of the Gandhian and not-so-Gandhian struggles of Indians for freedom.[40] What was impossibly wrong would be for one party to hog the entire credit.

Why did Nehru not allow INA fighters to join the Indian army? Did he fear that this would create confusion in the ranks of the Indian army? Was there really sufficient basis for him to assume that this would necessarily be the case? Even upon their return the INA fighters got involved with Gandhi in trying to quell the post-partition rioting in West Bengal.[41]

In revolutions across the world, once the revolution has been achieved and the revolutionaries cease power, there are those among them who seize power and others are left behind. This is a tragedy that has happened time and time again across the world, and sad to say, it would appear that India has been no exception. Bose would have been the first to accord primacy to Gandhi, but for the Gandhi acolytes to have ignored him, for Nehru to not have allowed the erstwhile Congress President to share a glory so richly deserved – that is tragedy beyond belief. It was never a 'this or that' situation. Should we stoop so low as to indulge in 'competitive' patriotism?

The British propaganda machinery made efforts at the time to depict the INA fighters as cowardly. Today's historians know how the tales of their ineffectiveness were exaggerated and part of the war propaganda. Although the British Indian army was numerically much stronger and therefore eventually prevailed over the INA in their skirmishes, with over 40,000 troops the INA was by no means a small force, and they fought with great courage and valour. As a matter of fact it is ridiculous to term the INA fighters cowardly; they were after all made from the very same Indian material as were the Indian soldiers fighting on behalf of the British; some had even fought for the British Indian army in an earlier avatar.

We will discuss, once again, the important issue of the much-needed corrections in the history of India's search for freedom in the last chapter of this book.

Chapter - 2

Nehru and His Strange Surveillance

I am not a shopkeeper and I do not bargain. The slippery path of diplomacy I abhor as unsuited to my constitution. I have taken my stand on a principle and there the matter rests.

Subhash Chandra Bose

Big Brother Nehru

Nehru was eight years older than Subhash Bose[42], so it is not inappropriate to think of him as the older brother, the big brother, so to speak. And he did watch over Bose's family, as records now reveal, like a Big Brother in Orwell-speak, though not like an elder brother. The surveillance that was mounted on Bose's family was far from innocent. Sandeep Unnithanwriting in *India Today* provides a telling instance of a letter written by Emilia, Netaji's wife writing to Bose's nephew Sisir Kumar Basu[43] where she is discussing her daughter Anita's physical development.[44] 'She (Anita) is growing in length,' the mother writes, 'and also quite well built, though by far not a fatty.'[45] As has been revealed by recently de-classified files, even a letter as personal and innocent as this would have been intercepted, read and photocopied by the Intelligence Bureau (IB) and only then would it reach the addressee, Bose's nephew. Why should Anita's physical development have concerned the IB? Wasn't this a serious breach of privacy rights guaranteed under the Indian Constitution? And how democratic was it of Nehru to have permitted, nay overseen and even possibly directed this high-handed surveillance on the family of one of India's great sons?

The Needle of Suspicion

Bose had been under surveillance for many years by the colonial British government, so Nehru apologists argue that someone simply forgot to remove the surveillance. This was however no burning electric bulb or leaky water faucet someone forgot to turn off. Not only was the IB carrying out surveillance, it goes without saying that they would have been sending periodic reports to the Prime Minister's Office.

How could Nehru have possibly done this to his old friend and comrade? It was not only letters that were intercepted. Bose's relatives – and he was a man with a large extended family – were shadowed and followed by the sleuths from the Intelligence Bureau. This spying was not confined to India; even when relatives went overseas they were tailed. It could have been a costly undertaking, but clearly money was no object here. Reports were prepared recording in minute detail who the relatives met with, and possibly even what was discussed at those meetings to the extent that the spies could successfully eavesdrop without blowing their cover.[46]

For over twenty years, copies of all letters sent to relatives by other relatives at the Calcutta locations were filed away and kept inside a locked cupboard in the IB's office in Calcutta. Following recently declassification of some papers this correspondence has now been moved to the National Archives.

The Family's Reaction to the Startling Revelations

Expectedly the family was shell-shocked at these new disclosures. Although Subhash's wife has passed away, Netaji's daughter Anita Bose-Pfaff is still surviving, working as an economist in Germany.

Anita is particularly shocked at how wide the surveillance net was. 'My uncle, Sarat Chandra was politically active until the 1950's and disagreed with the Congress leadership,' she reflects, suggesting that surveillance restricted to him may not have as troubling. 'But what surprises me is that my cousins could have been under surveillance, they had no security implications at all.'[47]

Grand nephew Chandra Kumar Basu reacted furiously. 'Surveillance is conducted on those who have committed a crime or have terrorist links,' he says. 'Netaji and his family fought for the freedom of the country, why should they be placed under surveillance?'[48]

Sisir Kumar Basu to whom Emilie wrote her letters (intercepted by the IB) died in 2000, but he is survived by his 85 year old wife Krishna Basu who has been a Lok Sabha Member of Parliament three times on behalf of the Trinamool Congress.[49] She finds the surveillance shocking, but also mystifying. House no 38/2 in Elgin Road, Calcutta where Sisir lived and which was under surveillance now houses the Netaji Bhawan Museum. Interviewed at that very location she explodes: 'Why on earth would they want to tail us?' The entire family was clueless about the surveillance. She recalled having her husband tell her that he suspected he was being followed, but that was before independence. Post-independence they never suspected anything; the IB sleuths were clearly very careful.[50]

The sleuths and their immediate supervisors may themselves have wondered about the reasons for their assignment. According to records some officials in the IB believed that the Bose family was planning to do a resurrection of the INA. The level of secrecy surrounding the reasons for the surveillance was so tight that even those supervising or actually carrying out the surveillance were not told why it was being done. These men from the bureau could not help but speculate as to the possible reasons and justification for the tasks assigned to them. This was a possible theory that came to the mind of certain individuals within the IB that could justify the high priority their seniors were giving to this issue. Perhaps, they imagined, there was an attempt to overthrow the government at the centre.

These officials misunderstood what was happening. In a 1949 letter that has now emerged into the public domain we find Amiya

Basu asking Sisir Basu, then a medical student in London to find out 'whether any of the German generals were once again active in West Germany, particularly Hitler's former chief of staff, General Franz Halder.'[51]

The letter is genuine, but the reasons vastly different from what was being imagined by those in the bureau. Some imagined a global movement taking shape, others thought there was an attempt being made to overthrow the government at the centre. Krishna Basu, Sisir's surviving spouse says: 'There was clearly an element of government paranoia here. My husband was only trying to gather material to set up the Netaji Research Foundation.'[52]

At the time, this letter and attempts to contact former INA loyalists (for the foundation) created great excitement within the IB. 'The subject,' one memo recorded, 'is now reportedly taking keen initiative in the formation of the Azad Hind Dal with ex INA men. It is reported that he has succeeded in influencing some prominent persons both in the state and in the centre.'[53]

Tailing Half the West Bengal Population – An Implausible Theory

Is it possible that the Bose family was under such intensive surveillance because of their leftward leanings? This is the improbable suggestion made by V Balachandran, former RAW special secretary. The theory he advances is that the British MI 5 was particularly interested in shadowing those who had communist views. So his theory is that this merely continued after the British had left.[54] It is true that the British did keep an extra focus on the communists; MI 5's counter-espionage chief Guy Liddel's diaries support this thesis.[55]

Balachandran states: 'The IB's obsession with tailing communist continued until Mrs Gandhi ended it in 1975.'

The RAW secretary's theory would hold greater credibility if the Bose family were not only left oriented but were political players of some significance at a national level. This was not the case. From the 1940's onwards the state of West Bengal was full of communists, and their sympathisers.For instance Jyoti Basu, who would go on to become the chief minister of the state, was well known for his communist views. Basu won his first election in 1952.[56] It would not have been physically possible to tail all the lefties of West Bengal. There was no evidence to suggest that the extended Bose family advocated a particularly militant brand of communist that could have merited such surveillance.

Further more if the snooping on Netaji's family was in fact simply of a routine nature the IB chiefs would not have bothered to examine the correspondence as closely as they did. Letters relating to family matters were produced before and examined by the senior leadership of the Intelligence Bureau in the 50's. Mr M L Hooda, (who subsequently ended up as the Director of the IB in 1968), and Mr R N Kao (who founded India's equivalent of the CIA) the same year carefully sifted through all of this innocuous material.[57] What was the need to put Top Secret and Very Secret stamps on the files? Doing so restricted the access of those files to only very senior officials. Clearly all this tasking came from the senior political leadership – the Prime Minister himself?

Trusting Nehru's Strange Surveillance

The surveillance on Bose's family would have been more comprehensible if Nehru as a person possessed a hawkish mentality or at least had an interest in espionage. If there was a great deal of espionage *anyhow* taking place by the government agencies, a credible argument could be made that Nehru possibly thought, 'Let's get the Bose family tailed as well,' just for good measure or even to satisfy some idle curiosity.

But Nehru was no Stalin or Hitler. He lacked the suspicious mind-set of a dictator. He professed to be a democrat, and there is evidence that he tried to nurture democratic institutions in the country. Historians such as Ramachandra Guha in fact contrast his governing style with the imperiousness of his daughter Indira Gandhi, who had scant regard for democratic norms.

The irony here is that there is evidence to show that Nehru even had a moral repugnance towards espionage – which he carried to somewhat ridiculous lengths. He didn't even wish to carry out espionage against countries who were spying on India! In his 1971 memoir, B N Mullick former chief of the Intelligence Bureau, tells us that Nehru 'had such a moral aversion to this work (espionage) that *he would not allow us to operate even against the offending country's intelligence groups operating from the shelter of their diplomatic offices in India.*'[58]

In other words, spare those who target India, and at the same time closely watch the family of a national hero.

A man who has something important to hide, the revelation of which may have far reaching consequences, will spend sleepless nights worrying, planning and making sure his tracks are fully covered. Could this possibly have been the case with Nehru, a colossus of Indian if not world history?

What was Bose's Nephew Up to in Tokyo?

Thousands of miles away in New Delhi, ignoring other important matters of state, Nehru was trying his best to monitor what Amiya Basu, Netaji's nephew and son of Sarat Chandra Basu was up to in Tokyo. The astonishing order from the prime minister instructing government functionaries in Tokyo to check what Amiya was up to was issued more than a year after the Shah Nawaz Committee was constituted. All the witnesses in that enquiry had already been examined between April to July 1956.[59] The government had categorically dismissed the Suresh Basu's Dissentient Report and full accepted the conclusions of the Shah Nawaz Committee. Still we find a worried Nehru snooping on the movements of Amiya Basu,of all people, issuing *direct* instructions as the Prime Minister to the Foreign Secretary to write to the Indian Ambassador in Japan.

The confidential letter dated 26 November, 1957 reads as follows:

'Just before I left Japan, I heard that Mr Amiya Bose, son of MrSarat Chandra Bose, had reached Tokyo, He had, previously, when I was in India, informed me that he was going there. *I should (sic) like you to write to our ambassador in Tokyo to find out from him what Mr Amiya Bose did in Tokyo. Did he go to our Embassy? Did he visit this Renkoji Temple?'* The respondent responded to say that Amiya had not visited either place.[60]

Why this inordinate curiosity?

Government Itself Not Sure Whether Dead or Alive

M J Akbar, the BJP spokesperson and journalist of some repute (although recently fallen into disrepute for his alleged misbehaviour with women) believes that the only reasonable explanation for the surveillance was that the government was unsure whether Bose was dead or alive.

'There is only one reasonable explanation for this long surveillance on the Bose family by IB, which reported directly to Nehru,' he asserts. 'The government was not sure that Bose was dead and thought that if he was alive he would be in some form of communication with his family in Kolkatta. Why would Congress be apprehensive about this? Bose was the only charismatic leader who could have mobilised opposition unity against the Congress, and offer a serious challenge in the 1957 elections. It is safe to say that if Bose were alive, the coalition that defeated the Congress in 1977 would have trounced Congress in the 1962 General Election, or 15 years earlier.'[61]

India's first Chief Information Commissioner Wajahat Habibullah is also mystified. Once the Freedom of Information Act started to be implemented, he started to receive multiple requests seeking information on the Netaji files. He says: 'The fact that the files have not been declassified when they should have been in the 1960s and 1970s has only added to the Bose mystery.'[62]

A Possible Explantion – Nehru was Actually at Sea

Could it be the case that Nehru's Big Brother watchfulness over Bose's family was because he himself was not completely confident that Bose had died? That of course leads to a further question. Why then did he try to resist an enquiry for so many years? Why did he continue to insist that Bose had in fact died?Could it be the case that the Soviets had told the prime minister that Bose had died while in their custody? Since Nehru hadn't actually seen the dead body, he wasn't one hundred percent certain that this was indeed the case. What possible motive could the Russians have had for doing this? Was it to make sure that India under Nehru did not switch its allegiance to the Soviets (or shift its so-called nonaligned position) towards the United States?

If Nehru ever dared to do so, the Soviets would release the cat out of the bag. In other words release Subhash Bose and send him back to India.

In other words Nehru expressed great confidence in Bose's death based on what he had been told by the Soviets. But later on as the years rolled by, and he ceased to view the Soviets through rosy tinted glasses, he began to wonder if the Soviets had told him the truth. Stalin was a crafty bugger. Was it not possible that Netaji was still alive, and the message sent to him at the time of independence that Subhash had died was a hoax? This thought started to disturb him at night.

Chapter - 3

The First Committee: Shah Nawaz Versus Suresh Basu

We wrestle not against flesh and blood but against principalities, against powers, against the rulers of the darkness of this world, against spiritual wickedness in high places...
Subhash Chandra Bose (quoting the Bible in the context of English rule)

The Irrefutable Logic of the Cause Itself

This is not a book about Netaji or about the INA although it does inevitably touch upon both subjects. Most readers will already have some idea about the cause that motivated and inspired Subhash Bose and the INA, It is probably still a good idea to provide an explanation in the eloquent words of Mohan Singh, who originally founded the Indian National Army in1942,[64]for why it made no sense for Indians to help the British in the world wars. He explains his dilemma in poignant terms:

I could not convince my conscience that it was right for Indians to shed their blood for an end which was not applicable to them. Britain faced with the imminent danger of invasion had declared that she was fighting for freedom, democracy and other high sounding principles. She besought others to come to her help. Even at this most critical period of her national history and when she was using India to fight for her own freedom, she refused to consider the question of India's freedom. Instead, she ordered the arrest of Indian leaders because they were considered guilty of asking freedom for India. Why should we Indians be fighting for a thing for others, the mere mention of which for ourselves was considered sufficient crime for the greatest of us to be put behind bars?!

Then why were we Indians fighting? The only answer I could find was that we were fighting merely as deluded, befooled, mercenary heroes at the expense of poor India for the sole benefit of Britain, thus helping Britain to keep India in subjection with Indian men, money and materials.[65]

The News of Subhash's Death

To now return to the subject under discussion. The news about the death of the 'springing tiger' appeared five days after the alleged crash. The announcement was made in Tokyo on August 23, 1945 that Netaji had died in a plane crash on August 18, 1945.[66] Why did it take so long for this announcement to be made? Netaji was not an insignificant man by any reckoning. Yes, they didn't have email and instant communications of the kind we have today, but telegraphic communications had been around for long, and five days was too much even by the standards of those times, enough to raise the smoke of some suspicion.

Five days is not too much though if the whole disappearance was a charade invented by Bose himself. This was after all a man who had disappeared from Calcutta under the noses of the British Secret Service – no mean achievement if we consider that there were 250 policemen who kept day and night watch on him.[67] It was therefore entirely possible that he himself had instructed those who helped him to escape to release the news *five* days later. Some would argue that this was Bose's standard operating procedure whenever he planned a disappearance: 'Wait for five days – and then release the information.' This would give him enough time to lose himself and prevent his enemies from sabotaging his plans. So, assuming he was going, say to Russia, he would possibly first go to China, and then after a day or so travel to the Soviet Union. Five days would be adequate.

Aside from the fact that news of his death was inordinately delayed, press reports from Tokyo and Taihoku(Taipei) published contradictory versions,[68] almost as if those in charge of spinning a story had not fully got their act together. When Mahatma Gandhi first heard the story of Bose's death in the alleged air-crash he dismissed it as sheer bunkum. The British too thought it was far too convenient for a noted war criminal – for Bose was such in their eyes, given his pact with the Japanese – to suddenly die in an air-crash just when they were rounding up all the alleged war-criminals.[69]

A Man Who Kept Disappearing

Bose's family members too found it difficult to believe the story, for he had done the disappearing act before; rather he had been doing it since childhood. His brother Suresh Basu recalled two such instances.

'When cholera was raging fiercely in a remote part of the district of Cuttack, he took training in its treatment under Dr Debendra Nath Mukerjee who was similarly inclined. As his parents were away from Cuttack and as his guardian did not permit him to go to the cholera affected area, he was not found in the house the next morning. As both he and his *ashramites* were of a secretive nature, two strong young men were dispatched to bring him back forcibly, and who, after wandering about a lot, managed to trace him in an out-of-the-place cholera-infected village, but they were unable to bring him back. He returned later on of his own accord, after he had finished his work there.'[70]

As a student too he continued to disappear. 'When he was a student at the Presidency College, College, Calcutta,' Suresh Babu recalled, 'he left his Calcutta residence without informing anybody, not even his mother and there was no news from him for about a month. He returned home suddenly in a bad state of health and it transpired that he was in search of a Guru (religious preceptor) and had trekked widely and in some portions (sic) of the Himalayan regions.'[71]

The Inexplicable Resistance to an Independent Enquiry

Given this background and history it was only natural that upon Indian independence popular demand arose for an independent inquiry into the alleged disappearance/death of Netaji. What was perhaps not as natural was the stubborn resistance from the side of the Government to such an inquiry despite the issue being raised in Parliament from time to time.[72]

Nehru's first stone-walling tactic was to argue that it was the job of the Japanese government and not the Indian government to institute an enquiry. It is indeed strange that the Japanese government did not institute an enquiry. It was not true however, as Nehru insisted, that since the alleged air crash took place in a territory at the time under the control of the Japanese, only they and not the Indian government ought to have carried out an investigation/ enquiry into Netaji's death/ disappearance. Since a very prominent Indian national was involved it would have been natural and appropriate for the Indian government to institute an independent enquiry and seek Japanese assistance, as necessary for that purpose. It is true however that the Japanese should also have carried out an enquiry into the crash for after all a high ranking officer, Lt General Shideo along with two Japanese pilots were also alleged to have died in the same air crash.[73] Indian investigative journalism was still to come into its own in the fifties and sixties for if any newspaper or scribe hadreally been interested he would have tried to contact the families of the Japanese alleged to have died in the same crash for corroborative evidence – and one can only wonder what such an investigation would have found!

Yes, there can be a counter argument advanced that it was the end of the second World War, the horrific atomic bombings had only just taken place, and there was chaos all around, but that chaos eventually settled, and there should have been an official Japanese enquiry into the air crash and the consequent deaths, even if a delayed one. Surely these are standing operating practices in the event of an air crash the world over now and even at the time.

Eventually, faced with persistent governmental apathy and intransigence on this count, prominent members of civil society threatened to constitute a publicly funded non-governmental Commission. An unprecedented step, it was bound to immeasurably tarnish the first Indian prime minister's image being carefully built up by the Congress party machine. At length, Pandit Nehru announced in Parliament on December 3, 1955, that an official committee would be appointed to go into the matter.[74] The Congress Party must have been forced to reflect how it would look if the public gathered up the money and a Commission headed by not just anyone but one of the most famous and reputed judges of the time, Radhabinod Pal, a former judge at the Nuremburg War Trials, started to hold public hearings.[75]

Did Bose Not Deserve A Portrait in Parliament?

Nehru finally ordered an enquiry, but after he had been left with no option. He paid lip service to Netaji's contribution to the cause of Indian independence but for very many years till someone raised the issue, Netaji's portrait did not even adorn the halls of Parliament where persons of far lesser eminence featured.

Jawaharlal was an intellectual, a sensitive man and an aesthete. Unlike his mentor Gandhi who made a fetish out of simplicity, Nehru with his specially tailored coat (that came to be known as the Nehru jacket) and trademark rose-in-button-hole loved the finer things of life and possessed a greater appreciation for art, music and the like. The absence of Netaji's portrait adorning the halls of Parliament could never have been an oversight. It was clearly a very deliberate omission. The portrait was installed in the central hall of Parliament only decades later once the issue was formally and forcefully raised. Should we only blame the Congress for the neglect of one of India's great sons? Today, everyone across the political spectrum wants to claim a 'piece of Netaji,' as the expression goes. As recently as 2014 though a report in *The Economic Times* observes that only one Member of Parliament, the Honourable L K Advani turned up to pay his respects on Netaji's birth anniversary! He, together with three former parliamentarians paid tributes and showered petals at his portrait which now adorns the central hall of Parliament.[76]

It would not be unfair to speculate that either Nehru did not remember Bose very fondly, despite his protestations to the contrary or that he could not bear to look upon Subhash's visage staring across at him whenever he addressed Parliament, which he so often did. Could it have been the case that Nehru, the Indian Englishman, looked upon Netaji like the British did, as a 'war criminal' that fought on the wrong side? Did he worry at the possibility of embarrassment when prominent British politicians visited the Indian Parliament and beheld the portrait of a war criminal mounted on the walls of the central halls of Parliament? Or, stretching the charitable explanation to an extreme, could it have been because looking upon that famous be spectacled visage made him emotional at the thought of the loss of such a dear friend? Surely this could not have been the case for by that logic even the portrait of Nehru's mentor, the Mahatma would have been excluded?!

Could it be that the emotional impact of having Bose's portrait facing him was troubling for some other reason? Why would a portrait of Bose have disturbed Nehru and made him uncomfortable? Conspiracy theorists and Nehru-haters may argue that Bose languished in custody in a Soviet jail in Siberia at the prime minister's bidding and so he, Nehru couldn't face Bose anymore, even in the form of a portrait on the wall. Whatever be the merit of such extreme allegations, could it be that Nehru did experience a degree of guilt – for some other reason – and this prevented him from allowing the installation of a portrait.

One does not have to be a conspiracy theorist to have a negative view of Nehru's reluctance to have Bose's portrait inside Parliament House. Those who despise Nehru and the Congress may also suggest that this was a case of pure and simple jealousy. This however raises a further question. Why would a popular politician, the prime minister, no less, be jealous of someone who wasn't even there?

The Appointment of Shah Nawaz Khan Instead of Radhabinod Pal as Chairman of the First Committee

Pandit Nehru provided several justifications for rejecting the candidature of Judge Radhabinod Pal as Chairman of the first Committee that went into the issue of Netaji's death/ disappearance. One of the reasons given by him was that this might 'upset the Americans.[77]'

A decade after the World War was over the Americans would hardly have given a toss whether the famed jurist Radha Binodpal presided over an enquiry or not. In fact if the Americans, or for that matter the British, had to be upset over anything it would have been over the fact that Shah Nawaz Khan was the Chairman of the Inquiry Committee – for as an officer of the INA, he was in a sense directly responsible for the taking of the lives of soldiers owing allegiance to the Allied Forces. Judge Radha Binodpal was not a war criminal in the eyes of either the Americans or the British. On the other hand, Shah Nawaz was a war criminal in the eyes of the Allied Forces, and had been tried and even sentenced to death! Had it not been for the reprieve he was eventually granted, he would lain beneath a tombstone standing somewhere, and been in no position to sit on the Committee, let alone chair it.

A second reason that Nehru advanced for rejection of the candidature of the famed jurist was that in his view Radha Binodpal had already made up his mind that Bose was still alive. This is unfair to the learned judge. The same could have been said of Shah Nawaz Khan who had publicly stated his view (prior to being commissioned to be the Chairman of the inquiry by the prime minister) that he believed that Bose was alive and would soon be back with his people. If anyone had made up his mind it was Nehru – that Bose was dead. If anyone had prejudged the issue it was Nehru. In March, 1952 response to a question in Parliament raised by HV Kamath he stated, 'I have no doubt in my mind – I did not have it then and I have no doubt today of the fact of Netaji Subhash Chandra Bose's death.'[78]

Where was the famous democratic spirit that was attributed to him by Indian and Western historians alike? Why is it that he could simply not tolerate a conclusion different from his own? Suresh Chandra Basu observed with great bitterness that 'as it appears that the intention of the government for holding this enquiry was only to confirm Netaji's death which was already the confirmed opinion of the Prime Minister and his government one fails to understand what the necessity was for obtaining the same opinion again and for spending so much public money for it.'[79] The other curious thing is that the famed jurist's public statement *about the necessity for holding an enquiry*should have affected Nehru so much, but an even clearer statement issued by Shah Nawaz Khan *that Netaji was still alive* did not have affect *his* candidacy.

According to Aurobindo Basu, Netaji's nephew (who facilitated his uncle's escape to Germany via the Soviet Union)[80] who appeared before the Committee the Chairman Shah Nawaz Khan announced at a public meeting held on 23 January, 1951 (Netaji's birth anniversary) that Netaji was still alive.

Chairman Shah Nawaz Khan did not recollect having said anything of this kind. He challenged the veracity of Aurobindo Basu's statement and demanded that he produce evidence that he had made such a statement. It was unwise if not foolish of him to have issued such a challenge for the proof was forthcoming soon enough.

On 8 June, 1956 Aurobindo Basu issued the following statement:

'The Chairman (Shah Nawaz Khan) has challenged the veracity of my statement and wanted me to produce some evidence that he actually made that sort of statement. *At that time I told him that thousands and thousands of people would come and bear me out on this point, if they were put this question whether Shah Nawaz Khan had made such a statement in these meetings or not.*

The Chairman had mentioned whether there were any reports on the same lines in the newspapers. I have gone through the old files of only two Calcutta newspapers, namely the *Hindustan Standard,* dated 24 January, 1951 and the *Anand Bazar Patrika* dated 25 January, 1951 and have got the following excerpts from the news published in the papers which are quoted here.'[81]

The excerpts make it clear that Shah Nawaz had issued a public statement before a crowd of more than a hundred thousand people that Netaji was alive.[82]

Nehru apologists will suggest that the background of the Committee members points to the great man's fair-mindedness and integrity. What better person could Nehru have appointed than a man who had worked closely with Bose himself? The master stroke was however to appoint Bose's real elder brother Suresh Chandra Basu as the third member. Which person in his right mind could challenge the selection and ultimate composition of the Committee? Out of three members, there were two stars here – Shah Nawaz and Sarat Bose.

The defenders of Nehru will pose the following question to those who seek to impugn the great man's integrity:

How could the prime minister, even assuming that he was 'cooking' the verdict, have been so sure that Shah Nawaz would fall in line?Did he even know Shah Nawaz that well?

Yes, indeed he did. Let us not forget that Nehru was one of the lawyers who were part of the defence team who were representing the so-called INA war criminals in the trial at the Red Fort. He would have had opportunity to meet and confer with Shah Nawaz in custody. Even after the death sentence was issued he would have been part of the negotiating team that sought a reprieve for Shah Nawaz and the others. At this time too, he would have been in close touch with his client, providing him with all kinds of assurances that he, Shah Nawaz should not worry and that through Nehru and the legal teams efforts, he would escape the hangman's noose? Faced with the prospect of death

Shah Nawaz would have begged Nehru to do all he could and disavowed all his past thoughts of a violent revolution. There was thus time enough for Nehru to bond with Shah Nawaz. Following the reprieve from certain death, Shah Nawaz would have looked upon Nehru as his ultimate benefactor and saviour, someone who had literally pulled him out of the gallows. Shah Nawaz became beholden to Nehru for the rest of his life. There were other counsel representing the accused, but Nehru was the man who could skilfully navigate the divide between the Indians and the British, who still held power. Whatever Shah Nawaz's loyalties to Netaji may have been, could he refuse to do the bidding of such a man?

Shah Nawaz Versus Suresh Basu

The Shah Nawaz Committee appointed by Nehru eventually confirmed through a majority decision that a) Netaji was dead and b) he had died in the air crash. Had the third member of the Committee also given his concurrence, perhaps the entire controversy would have come to an end there and then. But this was not to be.

Suresh Basu came out with a pungent and stirring dissenting opinion, in which he questioned not only the integrity of the other two committee members, but by implication the prime minister himself. Not unexpectedly the government struck back! Much was made of the allegation that dissenter Suresh Basu had signed a statement with the two other committee members to the effect that he was convinced that Netaji was dead.

Big deal! How could this assertion alone be used to discredit Basu, even if it were true? [83] Surely even if this was the case, Suresh Basu was entitled to change his mind?The Mahatma himself changed his mind every so often.If Suresh Basu changed his mind, he would not have done so for any benefit, but rather by making his dissent public he ensured that he would never hold high government office, at least not so long as Nehru was in power.

Shah Nawaz was quite the dictator in his dealings with Basu. 'You were,' he writes with anger in his telegram as if he was reprimanding his orderly, 'not authorized to go anywhere else to write any report stop no question of sending papers to you arise unless you return to Delhi stop as you are aware Committee's life extends to 31st July and report or reports must be submitted to Government by then stop unless you send whatever report you wish to reach me by the thirteen July will assume you have no submission to make.'[84]

Relations eventually became strained between the prime minister and Subhash's brother but at the start of the enquiry there was mutual respect. To be fair to Nehru, unlike Shah Nawaz, he never treated Basu with such explicit disrespect.

The Secretiveness of the Enquiry

Suresh Chandra Basu's letter to the prime minister at the very outset of the enquiry on 2 April, 1956 raised several valid questions.[85]

One of the queries was whether the enquiry should be open to the public. In his letter to Nehru, Suresh Chandra states that he had raised this issue with Shah Nawaz Khan and had been told that according to the Chairman 'all Government of India enquiries are done secretly and only reports are made public.'[86]

As a matter of fact the Indian nation itself had been in existence for a mere ten years by that time and yet the pronouncement was made by Shah Nawaz Khan as if he was referring to settled Indian government practice of a few centuries. And see how cleverly Nehru ducks the question. In response to Suresh Basu's innocent query he quickly realizes that it would not reflect very well on him, Nehru, the prime minister if he were to say that yes, government enquiries should all be held secretly. So he writes that if this is the Chairman's view that is how things should be. If Nehru had replied to say that he *agreed* with Shah Nawaz that would have been acceptable, but for him to say as the Prime Minister and as a trained barrister, that he had asked Shah Nawaz and had been informed that this was the procedure was simply not acceptable. Nehru knew (or should have known) far more about these things than did Shah Nawaz. This was not really a matter of giving respect to the Chairman but of not being transparent and disrespecting the Indian people.

The Dissentient Report

At the very outset in defense of Suresh Babu's report it can be said that he was clearly more independent than the other two committee members, who were both connected with the government. When he decided to write a contrary report, Chairman Shah Nawaz was not pleased. As Basu observed, 'my colleagues, *both connected with the government* have tried their utmost to secure and manipulate the evidence so that it could easily conform to the Prime Minister's statement in Parliament…'[87] Following Basu's refusal to toe the line, the Chairman, who still thought of himself as a commander, instead of respecting the difference of opinion, treated Basu not as a dissenter but rather as a deserter.[88]

Suresh Basu's dissenting report raised many valid questions and pointed to numerous discrepancies in the evidence and testimony. In my view taken as a whole, they successfully challenge the majority report. What follows is a sampling ofnumerous contradictions and discrepancies in the main report.

How High Did the Aircraft Fly Before the Crash?

Witnesses who deposed in favour of the crash that killed Netaji were all in agreement that the crash took place soon after the plane took off from the runway but thereafter there is a great and unaccountable variation in their stories.

The mind can play tricks and we can all forget details. A witness to a violent crime may easily forget whether the assailant was wearing a brown, maroon or redcoloured shirt, or whether the incident took place at two or three in the afternoon, but is it possible that a witness who survived an air crash may say at one time that the aircraft was a hundred feet off the ground and then say later that it was more like a thousand feet off the ground? It would appear highly improbable, by any account. And yet this is what happened in the case of Colonel Habibur Rahman star witness in the Netaji-died-in-an-air-crash theory.

He first stated that the aircraft was a few hundred feet off the ground but later changed it to a thousand feet or more! On the other hand, Japanese witness Major Kono maintained that after the plane took off it reached a height of about 30 metres, equivalent to roughly 100 feet and it was from that height that the plane crashed.There was just a gap or discrepancy of nine hundred feet between the two testimonies.

Expert witnesses contradicted Habibur Rahman's testimony.The crash would have been far more horrific according to expert witness Sastri, an Aircraft Inspector in the Accident Investigations Branch, Civil Aviation Department, who could be expected to know what he was talking about.

The photographs on record too simply did not match with Habibur Rahman's claim that the plane had ascended more than a thousand feet, unless the pilot had managed to regain some degree of control, which was not said to be the case. Suresh Basu's conclusions in this regard were reasonable.

'According to Mr Sastri,' he wrote, 'it would take three seconds to dash against the ground from a height of 150 feet and if it crashed from that height a 'major' accident would be expected. Taking Col. Rahman's version that the plane crashed from a height of 1000 feet and as stated by Major Kono that the pilots failed to control the plane, though they struggled very hard to do so and as no witness has suggested that the pilots had succeeded in doing so and as it takes only eight seconds to crash to the ground from a height of 1000 feet, the nature of the accident due to the downward mounting momentum of the plane could reasonably be expected to be something very horrible and shocking and beyond all imagination and nothing near what has been stated by the witnesses.'[89] Basu further observed that 'if the plane had crashed from a height of about 1000 feet with the pilots unable to control it, the impact would have been more than enough to finish all the inmates and that too beyond all recognition.'[90] It possibly did not require an expert to come to this conclusion.[91] Had the crash taken place from a height of 1000 feet, as claimed by Habibur Rahman, he would not have lived to tell the tale.

Weakness of Rahman's Fuel Tank Explanation

According to the testimony of Habibur Rahman who claimed to have been in the same aircraft Netaji was sitting next to the fuel tank. In his deposition he asserted this to be the reason why Netaji's clothes caught fire and not his own.

Suresh Basu, points out that in the bomber Subhash Bose was supposed to have been travelling in, there were no seats and seat belts of the kind that are available for instance in modern passenger aircraft. Only two proper sturdy seats meant for the pilots of the aircraft were installed. The other seats were placed on the floor of the machine. Furthermore, unlike the case with a passenger aircraft where there are side handles which a passenger can hold on to when the airplane experiences turbulence, in the case of a bomber there is nothing for the passenger to clutch on to in the event the aircraft starts to rumble and shake. Therefore, argued Suresh Basu, logically, following the rapid descent of the aircraft all passengers would have been dashed headlong into the cockpit, since according to all the witnesses the aircraft took a nose dive. Given the nature of the seats it wouldn't have mattered where you were situated.

'The evidence on record,' Basu writes, creating an impressive visual of the scene, 'is that as there were no seats, all of them, including Netaji squatted on the floor. As such it would be probable and reasonable to expect that when the plane nose-dived it would not be possible for any of them to retain their seats and they would all have dashed headlong into the cockpit or any other obstruction in the front portion of the plane. In any case, when the plane dashed against the ground on its nose they must have been hurled forward with the heavy and sudden impact and injured fairly severely also in the process, unless they were hanging like bats from any part of the plane, which they may have held firmly, but even in that case they would have in all probability lost their grip.'[92]

Unfair Treatment of Suresh Basu, the Dissenting Member

Certain papers were not made available to Suresh Basu, the dissenting member and he complained about this. The background to the unseemly and petty squabbles that took place is as follows. Instead of staying in official accommodation Basu chose instead to live with his daughter while writing the report, but she was required to suddenly vacate her government accommodation. He therefore needed a place to stay. The accommodation provided to him did not meet his standards and he asked to be therefore accommodated in the Imperial Hotel near Connaught Place. This was initially approved but did not work out eventually. As a result he left for Calcutta in a huff. It is true perhaps that Suresh Basu overreacted on the issue of the accommodation provided to him and perceived an insult where none had been intended. He allowed his ego to get better of him in this regard.

On the other hand it is also true that Chairman Shah Nawaz appears to have seized upon this departure as a pretext to not provide Suresh Basu with documents that would facilitate the writing of his report. No less a personality than Prime Minister Nehru got embroiled in the ensuing, unpleasant controversy. If Basu wished to see the documents, wrote the Prime Minister he needed to get back to Delhi. On the other hand Basu pointed out with justice that he was not demanding original documents. Copies could have been made and sent to Basu; the postal service was alive and kicking in 1956. What was the problem is sending copies to his address in Calcutta, as poor Basu had requested? Why insist that he stay in Delhi while writing the report? What additional value would this bring, especially since there was no mutual consultation involved following a falling out between him and his colleagues, and he was in any case writing a dissentient report. In response to Basu's letter to Nehru requesting the prime minister to intervene on his behalf so that documents may be made available to him, Nehru politely but firmly sidelined him, as if he wanted to let him know his place. Although Suresh Basu's request is clear enough (after all, how difficult can it be to understand that he is simply demanding copies of documents which he was clearly entitled to peruse as a member of the Committee?)Nehru responds with 'I have read this (the letter) and find it difficult to understand what you have written.'[93]

See the following extracts from Nehru's letter dated 13 August, 1956 (two days before the Independence Day of that year).

'The report (meaning the majority report issued by Shah Nawaz and Maitra) the evidence and the other papers were handed over to the External Affairs Ministry who now possess them. In the ordinary course the Ministry will examine these papers and will place the report before the Cabinet. If the Cabinet so decides, the report will then be placed before Parliament. That will mean its publication also. Probably the report will be placed before the Cabinet soon. It is likely to be printed.

This is the procedure and Mr Shah Nawaz Khan and the other member of the Committee have nothing to do with the report now, as the Committee has ceased to function. Should you however wish to send any kind of note we shall consider it.'[94]

Consider it to what purpose? The letter doesn't specify this, but one assumes that 'consider it for publication' is what Nehru must have meant. In other words, Nehru implies that Basu doesn't have a *right* to have his report published at government expense. 'We shall consider it…' leaves Nehru with the option of choosing to publish or not to publish. For Nehru detractors it could mean that if it is a poorly written report, we could consider it for publication since it would then indirectly validate the majority opinion. It was however far superior in tone and content to the majority report. Eventually Basu published the report on his own.

As regards the request for documents the prime minister is not impolite but dismissive. 'I am afraid,' his letter reads, 'no papers can be sent away from here now. If you so wish, you can come here and examine such papers as we have.'[95]

Inconsistent Evidence on the Site of the Crash

The Dissentient Report points out the discrepancies between the photographs provided by Col Habibur Rahman and the statement of other witnesses on the ground. The place where the plane is said to have crashed is described as 'flat country' by Rahman himself but the photographs show a hilly area. 'Col Rahman stated,' the report reads, 'that the photograph was given to him by the Japanese with the report that it was the identical plane, in which Netaji, he and others were alleged to have travelled and which subsequently crashed. The details shown in the photograph should have therefore more or less tallied with the statements of the witnesses, without which it cannot be considered to have any evidential value. It will be seen that it does not show the 'flat country' or 'plain open land' stated by Col Rahman nor does it show the airfield or the runway stated by the other witnesses.'

Did the crash take place a few miles from the boundary of the air field or on the runway? Even on this simple question there are discrepancies in the statements made by different witnesses.

According to Colonel Nagogaki, the crash took place on the runway; according to Colonel Rahman it was a couple of miles away from the boundaries of the airfield. Other witnesses give yet different and contradictory statements. As the dissentient report states: 'According to him (Nagogaki) the complete drama of the alleged plane crash was enacted on the runway and nowhere else. It is impossible for anybody to explain this definite statement that the crash and breakage of the plan took place wholly on the runway with the definite statement of Col Rahman that all this took place 1 or 2 miles from the boundaries of the airfield or those of the other witnesses that it took place elsewhere.'

Did the Plane Crash on Its Left or Right Side?

One would expect that there would be consistency at least on the issue of which side the plane crashed and which wing was consequently broken. There is no consistency even on this. Many witnesses testified that the plane definitely crashed on its left side and as a consequence the left side wing was broken. On the other hand we have Japanese witness Major Kono who categorically asserted that the plane crashed on the right side and as a consequence 'the right wing was completely smashed.'[96]

Who Removed Netaji's Clothes?

Most witnesses agreed that Netaji's clothes had caught fire. What happened thereafter is not however not at all clear. Different witnesses deposing before the Committee took credit for removing Netaji's clothes. Col Habibur Rahman stated that he was the one to remove Netaji's clothes, but other Japanese witnesses claim the credit for doing so. Obviously all of them could not have removed his clothes and we find more than one person is telling lies here. A person can forget the colour of the shirt he removed from someone's body, but he surely cannot remember performing an action – removing the clothes from someone's body – which he never did!

The question arises as to why so many individual Japanese officers claimed credit for doing so. I will answer this question a little ahead in this chapter. Suresh Basu expressions are sometimes garbled, but his meaning is clear. He observed as follows: 'Where Col Rahman and also some of the Japanese witnesses claimed to have individually removed Netaji's burning clothes, my colleagues disbelieved the statements of the Japanese witnesses who stated to have volunteered their services for that great Indian leader, for whom they had the highest admiration, and discarding the same, accepted that of Col Rahman on the sole ground that it must have been he, *who was most likely to have done so* for his 'beloved leader'.[97]Chairman Shah Nawaz Khan and his colleague were faced with the choice of choosing between several witnesses each of whom separately claimed to have undressed Netaji. They chose to believe Habibur Rahman instead of the other Japanese witnesses, but they could give no reason for coming to this conclusion other than the fact that Rahman was closest to Netaji.

Lest it be assumed that all the Japanese were discrediting Rahman's version en masse, there was also a Japanese witness who supported Rahman's testimony. This witness stated that he saw Netaji 'standing near the left wing of the plane with his clothes on fire.' He saw 'Col Rahman taking off Netaji's coat,' and then observed him having difficulty with removing the sweater. Even this witness cannot be believed however, for Habibur Rahman and other witnesses categorically stated that Netaji was *not* wearing a sweater![98]

How many clothes were removed? Some witnesses were more preserving of Netaji's modesty. A witness suggested that only the clothes on the upper part of his body were removed as 'his trousers were slightly burned.' On the other hand, we have two Japanese witnesses who testify to Netaji's complete nakedness following the burning of his clothes. According to Col Nonogaki, 'Netaji was stripped of all his clothes in the aerodrome and when he saw Netaji arrived at the hospital, he was absolutely naked.'[99] (Did they not cover his naked, burnt body with a blanket?). Major Kono states that his clothes too caught fire but in an exhibition of great presence of mind 'he rolled on the ground and put it out.'[100] Shortly after this, in a no-holds barred dramatic but unlikely visual, 'he saw Mr Bose standing erect, and completely naked near the plane.'[101] If Netaji could stand erect in such circumstances, was he really so badly injured? To add to this melee of contradictory testimony we have a Japanese medical orderly Mr M. Kazuuo stating that Netaji was fully clothed but that the 'buttons of his tunic were open and the front portion of his trousers was slit open with a pair of scissors to expose the burns on his legs.'[102] Later, 'his clothes were taken off and he was made to wear hospital uniform.'[103]

Was Yellow Paste or Olive Oil Applied to the Burns?

Witnesses cannot even be consistent in terms of the first aid treatment provided to Netaji. Some of the doctors testified that a yellow cream was applied to his skin. There was however a Japanese lady, a surgical nurse who claimed to have slept in the bed near the patient and applied nothing but olive oil on his body.[104] She also asserted that it was not possible to give him injections because he was so badly burnt. According to Mr Shah, a journalist with whom she spoke, 'there were three beds: Netaji's bed,

Habibur Rahman's bed and the third bed was for the nurse.'[105] This contradicted the testimony of others like Mr J Nakamura who stated categorically that there was no nurse.[106]

Why Would the Japanese Lie?

A question arises. Why would the Japanese tell lies more than ten years after the event? The air crash took place in 1945, and the depositions before the Shah Nawaz Committee took place in 1956. Even if we grant that originally the Japanese did somehow conspire with Netaji to perpetuate a canard about his death, the Shah Nawaz Committee was examining the issue years after the disappearance and alleged death. Japan was a free country at the time. Why would they need to lie? I can think of at least three good reasons why they would do so.

Firstly, if we examine the historical record we see that Japan had become free of American occupation not so long ago. The American occupation of Japan was officially dissolved only on April 28, 1952. There was thus only a lapse of four years since they had been returned to full independence. The Japanese may not yet have regained full national confidence, and at this juncture would not have wished to say or do anything that could potentially affect their relationship with the British or more importantly, their cousins, the Americans. The Americans had left, it was true, but they were now the acknowledged superpower on the planet and its 'special relationship' with the British was evident. Admitting that they, the Japanese, had attempted to fool both the Americans and the British (and more or less succeeded) could be politically awkward.

Secondly, the Japanese would not have wished to admit that they had lied previously even if it had been the case.

Thirdly, it may have been that Nehru had approached the Japanese and expressed his desire that they stick to their earlier statements.

Discrepancies Regarding the Nature of The Injuries

There are even discrepancies regarding the extent and nature of the injuries sustained by Subhash Bose. According to Habibur

Rahman, after the crash he noticed a deep cut on Netaji's forehead. Even a small injury on the face cannot be missed, for it is quite literally 'staring you in the face'. The cut was not only deep but four inches long. And yet none of the other witnesses mention in their deposition that they saw a similar wound.[107] The doctor who attended on Bose spoke of how his heart was affected but said nothing about how terrible his face looked. On the other hand we learn from Habibur Rahman that the face was so badly injured that he could not bear to have a photograph of his leader taken with that ravaged face. He decided instead to have a photo taken with the face covered.

It all looks very much like a cock and bull story.

No Witnesses From Family Members of Others who also Died in the Alleged Air-crash

It may be noted that there was no testimony from the relatives of others who had died in the same alleged plane crash. It would have been difficult to manufacture a family of the deceased pilot for instance, but no family members of other deceased persons were examined, or indeed ever contacted by the media or anyone else.

The Chairman's intellect Called into Question

It would appear to be the case that Shah Nawaz Khan lacked the training, background and intellect to sift appropriately guide the recording testimony and thereafter come to a fair and unbiased conclusion? His Two IC or second-in-command in the committee Mr Maitra may have been more discerning.

Suresh Babu mentions a certain incident in his report. A witness wished to make a statement with respect to the rectangular watch allegedly owned by Netaji. Now Subhash Bose was not known to possess any such watch but it was placed among his possessions recovered at the time of his alleged death. When a witness wished to testify in respect of Netaji's watch he was prevented from doing so by Shah Nawaz. The Chairman observed that witness testimony with respect to the said watch was already on record – and that therefore no further testimony was needed.

It was an open question as to whether Netaji ever owned or possessed a rectangular watch, and it was therefore important to get an additional perspective, if possible, from the testimony of another witness. The Chairman should rather have encouraged the witness instead of attempting to block him.

Suresh Babu writes on how in this instance the second member S N Maitra came to that witness's rescue, and explained to the Chairman 'as one would do to a child' how one witness might call a shirt green, another red and so on and forth and why therefore the witness should be given an opportunity to speak on the issue in question.[108]

What the Witness Must Have Meant

There were procedural irregularities that the Dissentient Report called into attention. During the course of his deposition a witness stated that Netaji's coffin was placed on a stool. Chairman Shah Nawaz instructed the stenographer to record that the coffin had been place on *two* stools. When the other committee member objected the Chairman pointed out that an eight foot long coffin could not, in his view, have been placed on a single stool.[109] Fair enough, but instead of confronting the other committee member Shah Nawaz ought to have pointed this out to the witness and sought a clarification instead of simply converting the statement, into what, in his view, *the witness must have meant.*

The Chairman may have had as his objective greater efficiency, in the military way, but this was surely not the way….

Committee Not Permitted By Nehru to Visit the Site of the Crash

Following the initiative taken by ordinary citizens across the country, more especially in West Bengal Nehru, finally gave in and constituted a government committee. And yet, he prevented this Committee from visiting the site of crash but putting forward what is evidently spurious and motivated reasoning. You do not need many reasons to veto a proposal; just one good reason is enough. The very many reasons that were provided by Nehru for vetoing the visit by the Committee to Taiwan were much like the excuses made by a child for doing a particular activity prohibited by a parent. A multitude of reasons and excuses are sometimes put forward because not a single good one exists.

In Hamlet, one of William Shakespeare's famous plays we have a character who speaks of a certain lady in this vein:

'The lady doth protest too much, me thinks.'

More than three hundred years later,[110] the same could be said of Nehru perhaps.

'The prime minister doth protest too much, methinks.'

Let's have a look at Nehru's strenuous objections to the Committee visiting Taiwan. This is what he had to say:

1. No diplomatic relations existed between the Formosans and our government. (The island of Taiwan was formerly known as Formosa).
2. In all probability that aerodrome with its buildings, runways etc no longer existed. Why was this so probable? Even if this was the case what was the harm in the Committee in visiting the site of the crash? In view of the significance of the enquiry was it worth saving the price of three return air tickets from Tokyo to Taipei?
3. The hospital being a Japanese military one had probably been demolished. Why would the Taiwanese demolish a perfectly good building just because it was used as a Japanese hospital? Initial rage at the occupation having passed, would they not rather prefer to divert the use to some other activity? Did India demolish all the military hospitals built by the British? In any case, my recent visit to Taiwan revealed that many Taiwanese are well disposed towards the Japanese.

4. The hospital and the aerodrome staff being Japanese were no longer there, and they, being at present somewhere in Japan it would *suffice*. Why should the Committee be concerned merely about 'what would suffice' as if the conclusions had already been formed? As a matter of fact typical for any colonial enterprise there would have been local Taiwanese staff at the aerodrome employed by the Japanese. What harm would be caused if the Committee went and examined witnesses in Taiwan?[111]

It's plain as daylight that Nehru was in panic stricken overdrive, and wished to ensure that the Committee not be permitted to visit Taiwan – because he was afraid of what the members would find there. Perhaps he was afraid that the Taiwanese government would inform the visiting Committee that there had in fact been no such air accident on that date.

Reading through Nehru's list of reasons why the Committee should NOT go to Taihoku one cannot help but feel be mused. Even Shah Nawaz made attempts, albeit unsuccessful for the Committee to visit Taiwan; it may have occurred to him that the reasons advanced by the prime minister for the Committee to not visit the site of the alleged air crash could dilute the credibility of the Committee's report.

Vaccillating Nehru

In this entire saga, Nehru exposes himself as somewhat desperate to not have any investigation into the matter at all, and then to sabotage the investigation once the committee had been appointed. One cannot accuse Suresh Babu of being unfair when he speaks of the prime minister's vacillations, hesitations and contradictory statements. As Basu observes, somewhat ironically:

'*One cannot help noticing that these are, after all, very curious and confusing statements and ever-changing decisions viz:*

The question of Netaji's death, being settled beyond doubt, and there can be no enquiry about that – was changed to – the only satisfactory enquiry that can be made, is by the Japanese government. Therefore, the decision – no enquiry –gives place to an enquiry by the Japanese government.

The decision, no enquiry, and enquiry by the Japanese government, vanishes and an enquiry by the Indian government takes place instead.

The opinion, viz, not in favour of setting up an Official Committee disappears and soon after an Official Committee is actually formed and made to function.'[112]

Nehru's view that the Japanese government ought to have held an enquiry was not completely 'off the wall' so to speak. Yes, they should indeed have held an enquiry but their failure to do so surely did not preclude the Indian government from carrying out one?

The fact that the Japanese government – comprising a people and race known the world over for their efficiency – did NOT carry out any enquiry itself raises some degree of suspicion. Why did they not carry out any enquiry? Not because they were confident that Netaji had died in an air crash but possibly because they knew very well that he hadn't.After all, two of their own citizens had also supposedly died in the alleged crash.So why was there no enquiry? The plot thickens as a crime novelist would say.

The Case of the Round Watch

In terms of their attire both the Mahatma (in his younger days) and Subhash Bose had a fascination for military service and attire. The Mahatma aka Sergeant Major Mohandas Karamchand Gandhi, who served with the British army in the Zulu rebellion wore military dress at the time[113] but eventually gave it up for homespun *khadi*. He wore the famous Gandhi spectacles as he got older. Netaji too wore round glasses – was it the fashion at the time? Gandhi famously wore an Ingersoll watch, costing just a dollar which he tied to his dhoti using a safety pin through which a *khadi* string made a loop.[114] Bose always wore a round watch gifted to him by his mother, which carried great sentimental value for him. Everyone close to Bose knew of this round watch which was never found; on the other hand no one knew of the rectangular watch claimed to have belonged to Netaji and found near the site of the alleged air crash.

Consider the following scenario: Netaji havingplanned his death by air crash understood that there would be questions raised about articles recovered from him following the crash. He possessed sufficient imagination to ask his collaborators to produce some of the things that genuinely belonged to him. Had the round watch which he habitually wore been recovered, it would, he may have thought to himself, in any case not constituted conclusive proof of his death. And he was in fact very much attached to his watch. Possibly it was too precious an item for him to part with merely for the purposes of corroborating his death. His death could surely be corroborated in other ways, he may have told himself.

Bring Back the Ashes, Said the Government

The Indian government was keen to have the ashes resting at the Renkoji Temple brought back to India from Japan. The ostensible reason was to pay homage to Netaji. Was it also the case that the authorities understood very well that once the ashes were brought back there would be some kind of closure to the controversy surrounding Subhash's alleged death, something it desperately hoped for? Basu writes on how 'it is evident that it is the intention of my energetic colleagues to have those ashes brought very soon, for reasons best known to them and also to our Government from the Renkoji Temple in Tokyo to India as they say that *the Japanese nation is belittling the Indian nati*on for not honouring the ashes of such a renowned Indian leader…'[115]

If truth be told, it was the Indian government under Nehru, and his successors, who did not give Netaji his due. The motivecunningly presented to bring back Netaji's alleged ashes – to honour the great leader – was a piece of pure fiction. The Indian government was belittling Netaji and the Indian National Army anyhow, and had been doing so for decades, ashes or no ashes.As film maker Sagari Chhabra's research shows us, INA fighters, who the country should honor as its war heroes, are ignored in Malaysia and Singapore and languish as stateless citizens in Myanmar.[116]

What was the Reason For so Many Discrepancies?

What was the reason there were so many discrepancies? Nehru apologists and those in favour of the Netaji-died-in-an-air-crash theory will argue that with the passage of time, witnesses are bound to forget precise details. Can one forget whether or not one undressed a burning man? And yet so many Japanese witnesses all claimed individually that they had done so. Can one forget whether it was yellow paste or olive oil that was applied to the burns of a war hero? Can one forget if the plane crashed from the height of a hundred feet or a thousand feet, or if it crashed on its right side or left side?

To my mind there is only one conceivable explanation. This was all a cooked-up business. It was a kangaroo commission from start to finish. The witnesses were briefed in general terms without going into the details. For instance they may have instructed that they have to say that the air crash took place, Netaji was burnt badly, and that he died as result of the burns. They were not properly briefed on what else they have to say, most importantly what they have not to say, and what other witnesses will be saying. And so during the questioning each one of the witnesses improvised giving himself a larger-than-life role in the fictitious story. As a consequence a multitude of witnesses each claimed to have been the one to have undressed Netaji. We have a certain witness testifying that yellow paste was applied; a second witness, a surgical nurse told the Committee that only olive oil was applied by her. It was possibly her own preferred lotion for third-degree burns, and she improvised accordingly while on the witness stand.

It was all an orchestrated performance beyond any doubt. The only problem was that the pianist, the cello player, the guitarist, the drummer, all the players in the orchestra were not playing their part in a single symphony, but were rather singing different and separate tunes, which explained the very many discordant notes apparent to any attentive listener!

As regards the reason why Netaji's face was not photographed at the time, it was not because of the injuries that were sustained but the likely explanation for this lies elsewhere. A world war was ending, and there were dead bodies all around (including hundreds of thousands at Hiroshima and Nagasaki the sites of the atomic bombings). Life was cheap and dead bodies were easy at hand. It would therefore have not been at all difficult to substitute another dead body of roughly the same size and height, have the face bandaged, take a few photographs, and claim that they were Netaji's.

It wouldn't however have been easy to find someone, at least in Japan who looked like Netaji. The right body could be easily found but a face that resembled Netaji's among mostly the Japanese war dead (wearing rectangular glasses?) Impossible!

Did Only Four Witnesses Say Netaji Was Alive – Or was the Number Fifteen?

Suresh Basu asserts that there was an element of careful manipulation by Shah Nawaz Khan the chairman of the committee. For instance he apparently made a public statement that out of 70 witnesses examined only 4 stated that Netaji was alive.[117] Basu clarifies that the number was more like fifteen and he lists the names of these additional witnesses in his report. Two of these witnesses, Mr K Satoh and Lt NB Das even contradicted Habibur Rahman, the star witness's statement and asserted that they saw Netaji take off in a separate plane *without* Col Rahman in it.

A Witness For The 'Fabrication'

There was a sharp disconnect between the evidence and those arguing in favour of Netaji's death. At least one of the witnesses, Mr SN Dutt, speculated on how the entire story of his death could have been fabricated.

Dutt commented: 'Sherlock Holmes would probably sum up the situation as follows: At Taihoku a minor plane accident was stage-managed by a deliberate collision with a boulder. This would support the police officer's statement of having seen the plane under repairs at the airport. Netaji's face was then heavily bandaged up to avoid identification to avoid identification and Col Rahman's hand was touched with carbolic acid. They were then rushed off to a hospital. During the night, the pilot, the navigator, General Shidei and Netaji the four 'dead' victims of the crash left for their destination. In the morning it was given out locally that Netaji had died at night and a covered dead body or an empty coffin was placed in a room at the hospital. Four days later, after the completion of further evidence, the death of Netaji was announced in a broadcast.'

This witness also speculated on the reasons why the Japanese broadcast his death even though Netaji was alive.

'If he were alive at the time, why did the Japanese Government broadcast his death? The answer to the first question is that the Japanese Government wanted to curry favour with General MacArthur after the actual surrender. It would have been an act of extreme meanness and downright treachery on the part of the Japanese Government to have handed over Netaji their erstwhile friend and collaborator to the Anglo-Americans and of this they were incapable as a self-respecting and a cultured nation. The only other alternative therefore was to broadcast his death after he had left and continue to support it with what manufactured and tutored evidence they could place before the Enquiry.'[118]

Corroborative Views By British investigators

It is worth mentioning that the very first British intelligence reports on the subject support the views expressed in the Dissentient Report. These reports were closer to the events and are in a sense more reliable.

Major Courtenay Young's of March 1946, seven months after the event[119] to his colleague points out that 'there are major discrepancies regarding the disposal of the body.' On the one hand you had Japanese military officer Isoda stating that Bose 'died at midnight in Taihoku hospital and that his body was flown to Tokyo by the Formosan Army.' 'Domei, on the other hand,' the letter continues, 'states that he died in Japan, while Habib-ur-Rahman states that he was cremated and buried in Taihoku.' The letter further points out: 'The discrepancy here is great, and appears suspicious. In addition if it is a deception plan it is one which has been extremely carefully and ingeniously organized.'[120]

W. Mckwright who worked for the British Intelligence Bureau wrote a letter just a few days earlier on 19 February which voiced similar misgivings. The letter reads as follows:

'My dear Young,

We have at last completed an examination of the information available here relating to the alleged death of Bose and the result is not entirely satisfactory for it reveals many discrepancies which, until clarified, make any definite conclusion on this incident a little doubtful. The SACSEA Commission no 1 report dated 6 November 1945 states….It is beyond doubt that he (Bose) had plans to go underground together with a number of selected friends of his movement. The earlier report from the Commission dated 18 October, 1945 suggested that the Japanese had undertaken to give Bose the necessary protection to go underground.

Yours sincerely

Sd W Mckwright.'[121]

Chapter - 4

A Tale of two Commissions

Our cause is the cause of freedom and truth; as sure as day follows night, that cause will ultimately prevail.

Subhash Chandra Bose[122]

The Justice Khosla Commission Under Indira Gandhi's Government

Given Suresh Bose's vociferous dissent it was not surprising that although the majority opinion of the Shah Nawaz Committee was accepted by the Government with alacrity it did not satisfy the general public. On the streets of Calcutta and in Parliament demands kept being raised for a fresh inquiry into the matter. Matters came to a head once again during the 'reign' of Indira Gandhi. Indira, Nehru's autocratic daughter has been held responsible by historian Ramachandra Guha for the decline of many democratic institutions in India.[123] Given her imperious, calculating nature she would have quickly understood that there was no need to have a three-member committee or commission. After all managing one person is always easier than three persons. Lessons learned from the Shah Nawaz Committee?

All that was needed was to choose that one person who would chair the Commission carefully. If he had strong judicial credentials no one would be able to quarrel with her choice for weren't judges, even retired ones supposed to be more independent than bureaucrats? That has been one of the criticisms made of the Committee appointed by her father; that none of the members had a legal or judicial back ground.

And so it happened that roughly one and a half decades after the first Shah Nawaz Committee had been constituted by her father, Prime Minister Indira Gandhi too gave the nod for a commission to enquire into the affair. The Government of India, in exercise of its powers constituted an Inquiry Commissions[124] to be headed by Mr G.D. Khosla, Retired Chief Justice of Punjab High Court.[125] This time the ambit of the enquiry was much wider requiring the Commission to inquire into *all* the facts and circumstances relating to the *disappearance* of Netaji Subhas Chandra Bose in 1945 *and the subsequent developments connected therewith.* The scope of the terms of reference could not be faulted. The Khosla Commission re-examined several witnesses who had testified earlier before the Shah Nawaz Committee; there were additional witnesses of course. Two of the members of the previous Committee, namely Chairman Shah Nawaz Khan and the dissenting member Mr Suresh Chandra Bose were also examined by the GD Khosla Commission. The Commission gave an initial impression of being very thorough, impartial and systematic. As a matter of fact Justice Khosla was praised for his intelligence and legal acumen by the historian Leonard Gordan.[126]

Eventually the GD Khosla Commission also came to the conclusion that

(a) Netaji had succumbed to injuries sustained by him in the plane crash at Taihoku and

(b) His ashes had been taken to Tokyo.[127]

The controversy did not however end.

There were three things that made the Khosla report somewhat questionable.

1. Did someone move the mountains?

Judge Khosla visited the airfield in Taiwan where the alleged crash took place. The Shah Nawaz Committee had not been permitted by Nehru to visit Taiwan,but there was no such bar placed on Judge Khosla. A former Bengali member of parliament, Samar Guha, was present with Judge Khosla at the site of the alleged air crash. A photograph on file captures Justice Khosla looking up at the sky as if trying to reconstruct in his mind how the accident must have taken place. The problem: a clear mismatch between the photographs of the alleged crash in which Netaji was supposed to have died with the location of the airfield.

How could this be explained? Perhaps the crash did not take place on the airfield after all. That would have been a plausible explanation but for the fact that almost all the witnesses who deposed before the Shah Nawaz Committee asserted that the air crash took place on the airfield itself!

This raised a valid concern that the old photographs of *some other crash* had been used before the Shah Nawaz Committee. A world war had raged and there was no shortage of aircrafts being downed and crashing to the earth.

In photographs taken of the crash where Netaji was alleged to have died the mountains were much further away. From the real airfield where the judge stood, the mountains were much closer! The view of Mount Everest from Base Camp is not the same as a view from Kathmandu!

Did someone move the mountains? This was the third, clearly untenable solution to the discrepancy.

Justice Khosla however refused to regard this as an important contradiction which called into question the entire 'died-in-an-air-crash' theory. It is interesting how the judge ignored the 'mountainous' evidence staring him in the face.

In not considering this important discrepancy, the judge relied on a legal technicality. In Indian courts of law, as is the case elsewhere in the commonwealth it is not enough to show a photograph to a judge to bring it into evidence; someone has to testify as to its authenticity and 'prove' the photograph. If a car crash takes place the official police photographer who takes photographs of the accident has to depose as a witness in court to have the photographs 'proved' in a manner of speaking. The photographs of the alleged crash had however not been formally 'proved' before the Shah Nawaz Committee and therefore Judge Khosla refused to consider them. With respect, he was relying on a hyper-technicality in the law here, despite well settled jurisprudence then and now that a Commission is not strictly bound by the provisions of the century old Indian law of evidence.

2. No enquiries made with the local Taiwanese authorities

The site of the crash was visited by Justice Khosla,but bizarrely the judge did not take advantage of his presence in Taiwan, to make further enquiries with the local Taiwanese authorities to confirm the existence of the crash as far as their own governmental records were concerned. The records of the Japanese colonial administration unless destroyed would have in due course passed on to the Taiwanese at the end of the Second World War, when Japanese occupation came to an end. No explanation for this omission or slackness was provided.

During the course of a visit I made to Taiwan in 2017, I made informal enquiries with the National Museum of History in Taipei and learnt that the bulk of records were preserved by the Japanese and handed over to the Taiwanese authorities. Both the Japanese and the Taiwanese communities are meticulous people and this characteristic extends to record keeping, be it in financial matters or relating to their history. I also found it interesting that the Taiwanese do not bear so much ill will towards the Japanese, as is the case, for instance, with South Korea.

To return to the omission by Judge Khosla in travelling all the way to Taiwan but not visiting local authorities to further his appointed mission to unravel the truth about Netaji's alleged death.

Why would a pilgrim visit the Ganges and not take a dip in the river? Why would a judge go to Taiwan and not use his visit and official position to make further enquiries with the government there on a matter of such national importance?

3. In Praise of Mrs Gandhi

A third thing went wrong – and this could not but fail to affect public perception of the judge and the report. The very same year that Judge Khosla published his report declaring Netaji to have died in the air crash he also wrote a book, that was in fact a hagiography on Mrs Gandhi.[128]It is likely that Mrs Gandhi would not have tolerated or rewarded anything less. Years later during the Emergency, some other sycophant wrote a book on her son, whose dictatorial mindset exceeded even that of his mother's, with the title; 'Sanjay Gandhi, the World's Wisest Wizard'! Judge Khosla's book is now, perhaps deservedly, out of print. When judges are perceived to be *chamchas* of the government, their verdicts too cannot be perceived to be fair-minded and independent.

There is an old saying that 'justice must not only be done, but it must be seen to have been done.'[129]

Background to the Setting Up of the Justice Mukherjee Commission

Another twenty-seven years passed. Public anger once again snowballed, and a fresh investigation was sought. It often happens in India that when the executive refuses to act on an issue of public importance, the courts step in. A public interest petition (PIL) filed before the High Court at Calcutta in 1998 sought urgent directions to be issued to the government. From a plain reading of the petition the internal convictions of the petitioner are apparent that a treasure trove of Netaji related documents existed, which the government not only refused to declassify but refused to even acknowledge existed.

Today we know that this perception was valid, but at the time, to an outside observer it may have seemed that a left-leaning, Bose-loving, hardened fanatic was making unreasonable and provocative demands. Had not the government already stated that it didn't have any more papers or documents relating to Bose? Everything that was there had already been made available to the previous commission/s? The petitioner's anger, conviction and extreme distrust is palpable in the very prayers of the petition which raised the following demands from the central government:

(a) To declassify and disclose all documents relating to Netaji Subhas Chandra Bose and the Indian National Army, and

(b) To make a categorical statement whether Netaji's name was still in the list of war criminals drawn up after the Second World War and issue a press communiqué to the said effect,

(c) Not to allow any agency or publisher or any person to publish the story of the death of Netaji Subhas Chandra Bose in the alleged plane crash on 18/8/1945

(d) To disclose the stand of the Government of India were Netaji to be found on Indian soil. Would the Government of India welcome him or hand over him to the allied forces for trial as a war criminal?[130]

Given the challenging, almost insulting tone of the petition and considering that there had already been two previous enquires on the subject of Bose's disappearance it would not have been at all surprising if the court had thrown the petition out *in limine* and charged the petitioner with wasting the court's time.

But, this was West Bengal.

Decision By the Calcutta High Court

The High Court was sympathetic to the petitioner's case and ruled that there was no need to deal with the various directions requested. It would be enough for the Centre to once more launch a vigorous inquiry onto the alleged disappearance and death of Netaji for the purpose of giving an end to the controversy.[131]

Following the court's decision, a unanimous resolution was adopted by the West Bengal Legislative Assembly[132] demanding that the Government of India make all necessary arrangements for availability of records and documents in and outside India so that scholars as well as the general public could have access to them.[133] The party in power at the time was a Communist Party of India – Marxist (CPI-M) led coalition.

It was 1998 and the Internet had arrived,but it did not occur to the Central government under Prime Minister A B Vajpayee that it would be in public interest to place the decisions of the Shah

Nawaz Committee and Khosla Commission online. It would take another fifteen years before that would start to happen – together with thousands of documents from hundreds of files, following declassification by West Bengal Chief Minister Mamata Bannerjee and Prime Minister Narendra Modi.

In hindsight, the West Bengal State Assembly's resolution was disingenuous to say the least. It smacked of hypocrisy, political opportunism, dishonesty and incompetence, for, as we now know, not only did Netaji-related files exist in the central archives which were however never released, there were scores of files in the West Bengal government's own state archives, gathering dust and mould. There is a proverb in Indian languages about raising a hue and cry in the city while the culprit is just next door. Thousands of papers in the state archives were, inexplicably, never released.

The State Government could have simply ordered declassification of the Netaji papers in its own archives with one stroke of the Chief Minister's pen. It would take another eighteen years or so before the Mamata Banerjee government would order declassification of 64 state government files,[134] stealing Narendra Modi's thunder, in part. It has to be said that at the time Mamata *Didi* ordered declassification, it was already clear that the Centre would soon be declassifying Netaji-related files in its own archives.

Ms Banerjee too was in power and chief minister of the state for many years, but did not think of releasing material available in her own backyard. Even if the material did not shed light on Bose's disappearance it could have had immense historical value. It could not have been assumed that files related to Netaji in the custody of the State government were any less valuable as compared with the files with the Central Government?

The resolution by the State Assembly called upon the Central government to institute a fresh Inquiry Commission in order to remove the mystery regarding the whereabouts of Netaji Subhas Chandra Bose.[135] This too was somewhat disingenuous. Bengalis who rail against the Centre must consider that they have also been let down by successive state governments for under the Commission of Inquiry Act, 1952 the West Bengal government too possessed the power to appoint a Commission.Under the law the 'appropriate government' which includes the State government has the power to appoint a Commission of Inquiry.[136]

It took seventy years for even the state government files to be declassified! Our government has sometimes been called a banana republic by its detractors. It may or may not be a banana republic, but it would certainly seem to be a 'nana' republic. In other words, overly paternalistic.

The New Commission and Its Terms of Reference

Previously, under Indira Gandhi, a one man Khosla Commission had been appointed. Now the government appointed another one-man Commission.[137] It acknowledged the widespread feeling among the public that the issue of finding the truth about Netaji's death still remained and the legitimacy of a demand for further inquiry into the matter.

Justice M.K. Mukherjee, a retired judge of the Supreme Court of India was assigned to conduct the enquiry.

Significantly, there was no longer a Congress led government at the centre. There seemed to be a ray of hope that important disclosures would be imminent.

What added to this spirit of optimism was the fact that the terms of reference for the Mukherjee Commission were extremely broad and could not be faulted. Surely the AB Vajpayee led government, which had raised a demand for full disclosure of the Netaji papers, when it had been in opposition would cooperate with the Commission and lend support to its work?

The Commission was to inquire into all the facts and circumstances related to the disappearance of Subhas Chandra Bose in 1945 and address the following issues[138]:

(a) Was Netaji Subhas Chandra Bose dead or alive?

(b) If he was dead, did he die in the plane crush, as alleged?

(c) Whether the ashes in the Japanese temple belonged to Netaji?

(d) Whether Netaji died in any other manner at any other place and, if so, when and how;

(e) If he were alive, his whereabouts.

A Calcutta Commission

The Commission considered Calcutta to be the appropriate location for its work bearing in mind that its very creation originated from the directions that had been issued by the High Court at Calcutta subsequent to the filing a public interest litigation. There was additionally the unanimous resolution passé by the West Bengal Legislative Assembly. Finally,from the list of witnesses earlier examined by the Shah Nawaz Committee and the Khosla Commission, it appeared that most of the persons to be examined before it were likely to be from West Bengal.

Perhaps the Commission also considered that with in Calcutta it would be more insulated from political pressure from the powers-that-be even though at this point in time there was no basis to assume that the centre would be anything other than cooperative.

Chapter - 5

Stone walling Justice Mukherjee

It is however for Providence to ordain who of us should live to witness the consummation of all our efforts and labours, and as for myself I am content to live my life and leave the rest to Destiny.

Subhash Chandra Bose

Inauspicious Beginnings

The beginnings were not auspicious and did not augur well for the future. The Commission approached the Public Works Department of both the Central and State Governments for suitable accommodation. The West Bengal State Assembly resolution appeared to have been only lip service or an exercise in public relations, for the State government was not very helpful in this regard. Neither for that matter, was the Centre.

As a consequence the Commission was left with no other alternative but to fend for itself. The Commission had to run from pillar to post or rather from Ministry to Ministry. Eventually, it found help at the hands of an unlikely friend: the Hon'ble Minister of Food and Supplies Department, Government of West Bengal. Formal occupation of the premises took place only on November 16, 1999.

Interested Parties Called Upon to Furnish Statements

At the outset,[139] as is usual, the Commission had a notice published in the newspapers inviting anyone who knew anything, either directly or indirectly of the facts and circumstances relating to Netaji's alleged death or disappearance to appear before the

Commission and make a statement. The same invitation was also extended to anyone having interest in the proceedings or wishing to assist the Commission in making its inquiry.

Sixty-three statements were forthcoming, with enthusiastic witnesses even filing supplementary statements, most of which were entertained. If anyone appeared disinterested it was the government. Somewhat curiously, no statement was filed by the Central Government or for that matter by the Government of West Bengal spelling out *their* respective stands! Under the law, all persons who are likely to be prejudicially affected have a right to be heard.[140] Big brothers were of course pretending to know nothing.

First Public Sitting

The Mukherjee Commission held its sittings in public in marked contrast to the proceedings under the Shah Nawaz Committee which were held in closed sessions. Even if we grant somehow that Shah Nawaz assumed that the Indian government was simply a replacement for the old British colonial administration, Nehru a trained barrister and a man wedded to democracy and by implication to transparency should have known better!

The Commission was based in Calcutta, but it also held public sittings elsewhere in India and even abroad. With respect to sessions in Kolkata and New Delhi, in order to demonstrate transparency, periodic Status Reports were issued providing details of its activities and the steps taken by it for an expeditious and meaningful inquiry.

The Commission held its first public sitting on March 23, 2000. On that date the Commission examined the statements filed by the parties, and heard them or any representatives who were present regarding the modalities to be followed in conducting the inquiry. Eager to get down to business, it passed an order directing the Government of India and the Government of West Bengal to produce various files and documents.

Nothing happened.

It was slowly becoming clear that it did not really matter that there was a non-Congress government at the center. At the state level too it was not the Congress but the Left Front led by the CPI (M) that was then in power[141].

Sharp reminders were issued from time to time by an increasingly irritable Justice Mukherjee directing the governments to produce more files and documents and comply with its earlier directions. Eventually some files and documents surfaced but many files and documents called for were not produced.

Evasions, Lies and The Destruction of Records

Its patience running out, the Commission now started to record how files and documents were not being produced despite repeated reminders.Despite being headquartered in Calcutta it made most of its file recovery efforts with the Central Government, possibly accepted the bona fides of the State government. On its part, either through laziness or for motives known best to it, the West Bengal Government kept mum and did not offer up any files on its own. Subsequent events have revealed that there were at least 64 Netaji-related files Government files are classified numerically as well as by subject matter. The Commission had been hard at work and managed to discover the numbers of certain files. When a precise file number is provided[142] it becomes difficult for even a government determined to be evasive to deny its existence – or rather that it had once existed. An important files number was provided and it was summoned by the Commission[143]. The response of the government was crisp but disappointing. The Director of the Prime Minister's office (PMO) responded, but only to say that the above file was not available[144]. It had been destroyed.

A Merry-go-round For Justice Mukherjee

Why the file had been destroyed, the judge wanted to know. Pat came back the answer. The files were destroyed as part of routine 'weeding out'. In any case, the Director averred, the records of Cabinet Proceedings are permanently kept in the Cabinet Secretariat. Unbeknown to her, barely two weeks before her assertion in a letter to the Commission Mr A K Paitandy, Director, Internal Security, Ministry of Home Affairs had categorically stated that there were no Netaji related files available with the Cabinet Secretariat!

This is what Mr Paitandy wrote:

> ".... In view of the fact that some of the departments/organizations have informed that they do not have any papers on Netaji/INA, there seems to be some confusion about filing of affidavits to that effect by them. In view of this fact and in deference to the directions/orders of the Commission, this Ministry is filling this affidavit on behalf of the following and I accordingly further affirm and state that there are reportedly no files/papers concerning Netaji/INA in their (the under mentioned departments') possession (emphasis supplied):
>
> (1) Cabinet Secretariat
> (2) Intelligence Bureau
> (3) Research and Analysis Wing"

Someone had either got their facts wrong, or being evasive, or simply telling lies. Either the assertions made in Mr Paitandy's affidavit was inaccurate or the PMO Director's averment mistaken that the file 'was destroyed in 1972 in course of routine review and weeding out of old records since records of Cabinet proceedings are kept permanently in Cabinet Secretariat, from where they may be procured"[145] (emphasis supplied).

Who Ordered the Destruction of Important Files

Bureaucrats all over the world hide things, although perhaps only Indian bureaucrats have elevated subterfuge to an art form. Before the Edward Snowden revelations, in testimony before the Congress, the US Director of Intelligence, Mr James Clapper lied about the extent of surveillance over American citizens.[146] He subsequently regretted his 'erroneous' statements.[147]

The problem, of course, is that lies and fabrications are not always carefully coordinated and properly orchestrated as became evident during the course of the Mukherjee Commission Enquiry.

Who ordered the destruction of the file? Once that person was identified, progress could be made – so thought the judge.

A letter to the Secretary of the Prime Minister's Secretariat called upon him to produce copies of orders to destroy files and documents concerning Netaji Subhas Chandra Bose.

Tracks had been carefully covered. The Director of the Prime Minister's Office (PMO) wrote back to say that no orders directing the destruction of relevant files or documents could be located.[148] There was, however, a record of the actual destruction andshe enclosed a copy of the relevant page of the File Register showing destruction of a particular file in 1972.

Absurd and Disingenious Defences

Mean while the Cabinet Secretariat wrote to the Secretary of the Commission to say that their organization had no record relating to the events as it was formed only on September 21, 1968 i. e after the alleged air-crash. How should that have mattered? By this logic the Indian government should have no records with it related to any events before independence. It was no one's case that the British shipped away all pre-independence the files to London, or destroyed all files prior to departure (although they may have destroyed some files relating to sensitive issues).

Today we know that they left hundreds of files related to Netaji. Moreover the file in question had been destroyed in the PMO's office only in 1972, four years after the formation of the Cabinet Secretariat!

The Timing of the Destruction

The irony is that that particular file is said to have been destroyed in 1972, *during the course of an ongoing enquiry*. The

Khosla Commission inquiry commenced in 1970 and concluded only in 1974.At that time Prof. Samar Guha, Member of Parliament, wrote a letter to Indira Gandhi, the then prime Minister of India,[149]wherein he requested the Prime Minister to have the matter investigated and forward the file, if not destroyed, to the Commission. Along with the letter he enclosed a copy of the notings on the file.

Mrs Gandhi wrote back to say, inter alia, that the 'file contained only copies of certain documents which are still available in other files' and that is why 'the file was destroyed.'[150]

What Happened to the File – Three Possibilities

Eventually Justice Mukherjee came to the unavoidable conclusion that the stand taken by the various ministries, the Cabinet Secretariat and the government in general was evasive and unfathomable.

Three possibilities existed with respect to that all important file.

(a) Copies of the documents in the original missing file *did* exist but the government was too lazy or inefficient to track them down despite the Commission's repeated efforts (Highly unlikely, but not impossible).

(b) Copies of the documents did exist but the Cabinet Secretariat was under strict orders from political higher ups all the way up to the Prime Minister's Office, NOT to provide the file to the Commission (Entirely possible).

(c) The original and all copies had been destroyed following instructions from the highest political office. Human beings can be destroyed for political advantage; this was a mere file, even if a highly important one (Entirely possible).

An Extraordinary Declaration: Morarji Desai on the Shah Nawaz and G Khosla Reports

What happened with some important files could have

happened with others as well. Is it possible that ALL important files relevant to Netaji's disappearance were not destroyed? Some argue that the destruction of files with crucial and significant information was started in Prime Minister Nehru's time and completed during the time his daughter Indira Gandhi held the same high office?

It appears that even after Indira Gandhi lost power in the 1977 elections, important material still existed which rebutted the died-in-an-air-crash theory. That this was the case becomes clear from the statement of Prime Minister Morarji Desai made in1977 the very year the Indira Gandhi led Congress Party was thrown out of power as the Indian public responded in no uncertain terms to the imposition of an Emergency.

The Janata Party, an anti-Emergency coalition swept into power and took charge.Following a motion on August 3, 1977 by Prof. Samar Guha in Parliament (Lok Saba) Mr Morarji Desai, the then Prime Minister of India, made the following extraordinary statement:

> "There have been two enquiries into the report of the death of Netaji Subhas Chandra Bose in the air-crash on 18th August 1945 at Taihoku airfield during his air-journey to Manchuria, one by a Committee presided over by Maj. General Shah Nawaz Khan and the second by a one-man Committee (sic) of enquiry headed by Shri G.D. Khosla, retired Judge of the Punjab High Court. The Majority report of the first Committee and Shri Khosla held the report of the death as true. *Since then, reasonable doubts have been cast on the correctness of the conclusions reached in the two reports and various important contradictions in the testimony of witnesses have been noticed, some further contemporary official documentary records have also become available. In the light of those doubts and contradictions and those records, Government find it difficult to accept that the earlier conclusions are decisive."*[151] (Emphasis and italics mine).

Yet sadly, while Prime Minister Desai raised the issue in Parliament, it did not occur to him to simultaneously issue instructions declassifying the information and files on the basis of which he had made his assertions.

No Such Records Could Be Found, They Said at the Time

Many new facts have now come to light. It is apparent today that even senior bureaucrats were guilty of deception when they claimed that no files related to Netaji existed. This was not the case of a few odd files that were not being produced before the Mukherjee Commission. As we now know there were actually *hundreds* of such files….

On what basis did Morarji Desai Prime Minister of India make his remarkable statement on the floor of the house? What were the 'further contemporary documentary records' that had become available? How was the prime minister of the country able to state so categorically that 'the Government finds it difficult to accept that the earlier conclusions are decisive'?

Despite Desai's clear, forthright and unequivocal statement, at the time that the Mukherjee Commission made its inquiry, the government in power at the center, despite being a BJP led government, was in full denial mode.

Jarnail Singh, a Joint Secretary with the PMO, filed an affidavit on December 18, 2001 wherein he averred, inter alia, 'no such records could be found in this office'. Due searches were made, his statement affirmed, to trace any 'contemporary official documentary records' that may have formed the basis of the statement of Prime Minister Desai on the floor of the Parliament on August 28, 1978[152]. His office was not in a position to provide any clarification or explanation regarding the circumstances under which Desai had made his statement.

How to Handle Evasive and Lying Bureaucrats

What can be done when a senior bureaucrat tells a lie, withholds information, or avoids producing a document? The

Commission has been given powers of a civil court in requiring the production of documents, and requisitioning any public record.[153]

What would be the point of giving the Commission power to receive evidence on affidavits, if it could not prosecute someone for furnishing, what appears to it, to be a false affidavit? Powers have therefore been given to Commissions under five separate offences under the Indian Penal Code, 1860 to prosecute those who tell lies, withhold information or fail to produce documents.[154] Its proceedings are deemed to be the equivalent of judicial proceedings for the purposes of imposing penal sanctions.[155] The omission to produce a document that a person is legally bound to put forward, is punishable by six months imprisonment;[156] the fabrication of evidence is punishable by up to seven years imprisonment.[157]

Could the Commission have wielded the threat of prosecution more aggressively to prevent government officials from resorting to obfuscation, prevarication and evasion? Something can clearly be done. The Mukherjee Commission tried persuasion and persistence but perhaps did not exert its full authority to force bureaucrats to be more cooperative and forthcoming. The law provides that any one telling a lie before it could be prosecuted.

The Freedom of Information Act

The Mukherjee Commission cannot be faulted on its persistence. It made repeated requests to the government for production of files and documents, but the government kept pussyfooting, all the while making one excuse after another. What a high-ranking Commission and former Supreme Court judge could not achieve in terms of disclosures was accomplished instead by Right to Information activists.[158] As a result of these efforts many secret and previously withheld documents finally saw the light of day.

The efforts by these journalists and RTI activists alone would not have worked had it not been for the creation of an authority overseeing the proper functioning of the law as well as the punitive measures provided for in the Right to Information Act, 2002. In ancient times, a Roman emperor is reported to have said that you can either raise people to the good and the useful or – you can subdue them. It appears that our cowardly bureaucrats only fear their bosses and must have another greater fear casting its large shadow – that of possible incarceration in jail – for them to do their duty. The evidence shows that India's babus and super-babus feared punishment under the Freedom of Information Act, 2002 and but cared two hoots for the repeated pleas and exhortations of a former judge of the Supreme Court, that is to say Justice Mukherjee.

Concealment Across the Board By Senior Bureaucrats

Home Ministry

Within the Ministry of Home Affairs, Ms. Sangita Gairola, a Joint Secretary in that Ministry, filed an affidavit on December 20, 2001wherein she stated, inter alia, that no 'contemporary official records' could be located in their Ministry. They Ministry had taken up the matter with the Prime Minister's Office with a request to trace the relevant records at their end.[159]

Ministry of External Affairs

The Ministry of External Affairs separately wrote to the Commission the same month to say that they had checked all records available in their Ministry but could not locate any document referred to in the former Prime Minister's statements.[160]An affidavit was filed by Jayant Prasad, a Joint Secretary of that office to the effect that no such document was available with them.

Cabinet Secretariat

The response from the Cabinet Secretariat completed the circle. An affidavit by a Joint Secretary in the Research and Analysis Wing swore that there were no records relating to the statement of the late Prime Minister made on the floor of the Parliament on August 28, 1978.

What Did Morarji Know?

Fortunately for these evasive bureaucrats and their collective amnesia, Prime Minister Morarji Desai was no longer alive to come forward then and reveal with Gandhian forthrightness what had led him to make that particular statement. It is difficult to believe that the Prime Minister of the country would make an ill-considered and inaccurate statement on the floor of the Parliament challenging the conclusions of two government sponsored enquiries, unless he had a firm basis for doing so. Apart from the damage to his reputation Prime Minister Desai would have invited the risk of breach of privilege in the event of non-availability of the contemporary official records referred to by him. The firm denial that such records existed by senior officers of various concerned ministries undoubtedly put a spoke in the wheel of the Mukherjee Commission inquiry.

It is possible of course that the bureaucrats were not telling lies or being evasive, and they really could not find the files. If this was really the case it can only mean that those particular files had been destroyed between the time Morarji Desai made his statement in 1977 and the swearing in of AB Vajpayee in 1999.

A great deal can happen in 22 years, and it can be plausibly argued that Prime Minister Morarji Desai's statement created panic and sent shivers down the spine of certain individuals.

Those men and women breathed a sigh of relief that Desai confined himself to stating that materials existed due to which '*reasonable doubts have been cast on the correctness of the conclusions reached in the two reports* (Shah Nawaz Committee and Khosla Commission).' Therefore, at the very first opportunity that presented itself when, for instance, Indira Gandhi romped back to power in the next elections following the failure of the Janata Party political experiment, that explosive material lying on the pages of the never produced files Desai had relied upon was destroyed.

Shocking: Even Records Available To Earlier Enquiries Not Provided!

Shockingly, even records available to earlier enquiries were not made available to the Justice Mukherjee Commission. What possible excuse could there be for this wanton disrespect of the Commission? No wonder the Commission came to the conclusion that the government had something to hide.

Complete records of the Khosla Commission (including witness testimony) were not made available to the Mukherjee Commission till very late in the day. This was not oversight but deliberate. Such withholding of documentation that should, in fact, have been placed in the public domain certainly lends credence to the hypothesis that the earlier Committee findings were predetermined by the government, so it didn't really matter what material lay before it. The results were already known by the powers-that-be.

Justice Mukherjee was however an 'unknown quantity' as the expression goes. The government of the day could not be sure what he would conclude **on the basis of the same material that had been provided to the Khosla Commission.** Perhaps a high level secretive internal assessment came to the conclusion that the earlier material, if provided to the Justice Mukherjee Commission could lead it to draw conclusions that supported the thesis that Netaji had *not* died in the alleged air crash. Did the government fear that the very same records and material could lead to completely different inferences by Justice Mukherjee? Would the judge critique earlier reports from the Shah Nawaz Committee and the Justice Khosla Commission?

Justice Mukherjee observed with resigned sadness: '***Records of the entire proceedings of the Khosla Commission and a large number of the documents exhibited before it, though called for by this Commission from time to time since August 18, 2000, were not furnished by the Government of India.***'

And then see the subsequent shamelessness of our politicians and law-makers. Home Minister Shivraj Patil had the gall to call in the judge and lecture him on wasting public money and resources.[161] It was Shivraj Patil's own ministry that had been pussyfooting and delaying the production of relevant records for months. Eventually the Commission received copies of the earlier proceedings in 'Argument Session' only. Did it finally dawn on someone in the government how this withholding of documents would look to any bipartisan, neutral observer?

Even then copies of the proceedings were made available but not all the documents placed before the earlier Commission and Committee. To retrieve the Khosla Commission documents, at one point in the middle of February2003, a desperate Justice Mukherjee even sent one of the officers working for the Commission to New Delhi. The officer so deputed examined the files and documents as produced before him by the MHA officials and the officials of the Internal Security Division of MHA.[162]He managed to find a list of the exhibits of the Khosla Commission. *However none of the documents mentioned in that list, though asked for by the officer, could be made available to him for scrutiny!*[163]

Truth, as they say, is stranger than fiction.

The Death of Witnesses

In a previous chapter we spoke of the great inconsistencies between the statements of different witnesses who testified before the Shah Nawaz Commission. Was the Mukherjee Commission able to examine any surviving witnesses?

Japanese life expectancy is among the highest in the world. Indians lag behind, though less so now than previously. In 1945, when Netaji disappeared, the life expectancy of Indians was astonishingly low by today's standards.[164] By the time the Mukherjee Commission got down to business the following year nearly fifty-five years had elapsed since that alleged air crash. A witness who was 25 years old then would be 80 in the year 2000!

It is therefore not at all surprising that the Commission found that 'owing to the long passage of time a considerable number of witness whose evidence have been helpful to this inquiry were found to be either dead or untraceable or too old and infirm to depose'.[165]

Despite this limitation the Commission was able to examine 131 witnesses in and outside India.

The Argument in Defence of Nehru and Mrs Gandhi

Congress apologists point out that if Nehru and Mrs Gandhi had really wished to destroy Netaji related files, there would not in that case be hundreds of files still in existence that the Modi government started to declassify. If Nehru and Mrs G were really all that manipulative, so this argument runs, why would they have not have simply destroyed ALL the files?

There is a counter-argument. The very fact that there were hundreds of files and thousands of documents lying within those files made their destruction difficult. A parliamentarian was able to pick up on the destruction of a single file and address a pointed question to Mrs Gandhi, embarrassing her. What would happen ifinformation on the destruction of hundreds of files were to be leaked?

India was not a police state and it simply wasn't possible to destroy all that many documents without word getting out. So, it was far better strategy to simply not to make files available rather than order their destruction.

In the event of a mass destruction of files and documents the possibility of a scandal in that case breaking through was immense. It was better to tread softly. The other thing was that there was possibly nothing in those documents that would shed light on the truth or otherwise of the air crash. Most documents were likely to be dated much prior to that alleged incident. Why risk public exposure on account of the destruction of documents that were in any case unlikely to be helpful to the enquiry that was being held? Besides weren't the enquiries already cooked and pre-determined – both during Nehru and Indira Gandhi's time?

Chapter - 6

The Crouching Dragons

It is not Japan who we are helping by waging war on you (the Americans) and our mortal enemy – England. We are helping ourselves, we are helping Asia...

Subhash Chandra Bose[166]

Searching Across the Globe: United States, United Kingdom, Taiwan, Thailand and Russia

A towering, dynamic and globe-trotting figure in his lifetime, there was a possibility of finding bits and pieces of the puzzle behind Subhash Bose's alleged death or disappearance in different parts of the world. Faced with stonewalling tactics by the government, on his part Justice Mukherjee decided to leave no stone unturned to unravel the truth. He determined that he would look outside the country, and hoped that there would be no such similar, desperate attempts to cover things up.

The Commission visited libraries and government offices in the United Kingdom, and the United States. In Japan it visited the Renkoji Temple. The Shah Nawaz Committee's request to visit the site of the alleged crash in Taiwan had been turned down by Prime Minister Nehru. The Mukherjee Commission was however granted an opportunity to visit Taiwan. On the way back from Taipei the Commission visited Bangkok and examined a witness there. Finally the Commission also visited the Russian Federation to examine witnesses and inspect records in various government archives.[167]

Would the Commission's overseas travels bring it any closer to finding out the truth of what had happened to one of India's greatest sons? What kind of encounter would he have with the erstwhile Crouching Dragons that once bandied together against India's Springing Tiger?

Crouching Dragon – the English

The Mukherjee Commission went to England to see if it could discover and study files that related to Netaji that could potentially provide information regarding his alleged death. Justice Mukherjee spent time examining records available at various libraries and government offices. During the course of the inspection of such records, he was not given access to two files, as they were marked 'closed'.

Justice Mukherjee believed those files could contain useful information, and approached the Foreign and Commonwealth Office (FCO) of the British Government for access to be granted. The FCO handed over a note explaining that certain papers from the files of the Intelligence and Security Agencies were withheld from release by the Lord Chancellor in accordance with relevant provisions of the UK's Public Records Act, 1958.[168]

Using his personal connections Justice Mukherjee thereafter met Lord Peter Archer,[169] and requested him to persuade the Lord Chancellor to grant access to the files. Lord Archer promised to help, but ultimately failed in his persuade the authorities. He suggested that there might be greater success if diplomatic representations were made between the two Governments.[170]

Getting the hint, Justice Mukherjee approached the Indian Minister of External Affairs requesting him to take up the matter at a government to government level with the Lord Chancellor. The minister assured the judge of necessary action and follow up.[171] Subsequently the Commission received a letter from a Joint Secretary of the Ministry[172] enclosing a communication from the British Government addressed to the Indian High Commission.[173] The UK government merely reiterated its earlier stand regarding the request for granting access to the files in question. It expressed its inability to say anything more helpful on the issue – and that was the end of that.

The British were not being cautious without reason. At the same time their secretiveness did not necessarily mean that those files contained information relevant to Netaji's alleged death in an air-crash. Other skeletons in the English cupboard in a Netaji related context could have tumbled out! For instance, they would have wished to keep concealed such as, for instance, the assassination attempts made on Subhash Bose.

If Fidel Castro represented an ideological foe for the Americans in the 60's and 70's (with the numerous failed assassination attempts by the CIA) Bose had represented a far greater challenge for the British a few decades earlier.

Castro's threat to American capitalism was far exaggerated, as was the case with Vietnam, but Bose, on the other hand, was a man who could, through his actions, stoke the fires of rebellion in the British Indian army. This was a truly fearsome prospect that the British dreaded ever since its Indian forces had revolted in 1857, sparking off what some would call the first Indian War of Independence.

Crouching Dragon – the Americans

The Americans and the British played for the same team in the Second World War. Bose played for the opposite side. If the British wished to eliminate Bose, for which there exists ample evidence, it could have counted on American support. The Americans would not have hesitated to offer full assistance.

Gandhi, Nehru and the Indian National Congress may not have fully appreciated the truth in Bose's assertion that 'the enemy of my enemy is my friend' but the British and Americans clearly understood the converse: the friend of my enemy is also my enemy!

But many decades had rolled on since those days. It was a new world now. Would the Americans still behave like a crouching dragon?

The United States was an obvious place to search for records that could shed light on Bose's death or disappearance. Upon the conclusion of the war it was the United States and not the English that occupied Japan. The US presence in Japan continued for many years. In the aftermath of the war, the Americans would not have trusted the Japanese one bit. Memories of Pearl Harbour were still fresh, together with collective American guilt over the atomic bombings– and fear of retribution for that horrific crime against humanity? American spies remained active on the ground in Tokyo and major Japanese cities.

As collaborators in the war effort, the British shared intelligence with the Americans. American Intelligence eventually took the shape of the Central Intelligence Agency (CIA), established on 18 September 1947. Earlier wartime records would have been subsequently transferred to the CIA, and could potentially reveal information that shed light on Netaji's disappearance or death. Unlike India where secrecy on Netaji related government files continued unabated for seven decades altogether, in the US, confidential information is subsequently declassified within a more reasonable time frame.

Against this back drop the Commission asked the Ministry of External Affairs to request the Americans to make available to it all declassified documents on Netaji Subhas Chandra Bose/INA in their possession – including those with the CIA, and the McArthur papers.[174] The Ministry of External Affairs tasked the Embassy of India in USA with the necessary follow up.[175]

The Director of Textual Archives Services Division of USA provided a heartening response to enquiries made by the Indian Embassy. The Ministry of External Affairs took up the matter with the American Embassy in India. The American Embassy in India communicated this positive response to the Indian government.[176] There was however still a problem: records were scattered all over the United States.

It wasn't practical for the Commission to spend months visiting different research centres where records existed given the strict time lines under which it was operating. The Commission therefore requested the Indian government to hire qualified scholars to undertake archival research at American repositories of historical documents on Bose.[177] Reminders issued by the Commission were ignored.[178]

The attempts to uncover Netaji related information in the US met with no success.

Crouching Dragons – Russia?

A theory has long done the rounds that Netaji escaped from Japan and went off to Russia, to escape the clutches of the Allied Forces out to arrest Indian National Army (INA) members. The sought after Russian refuge turned into a prison sentence for Bose. In this version of events, the Russian bear did not provide a comforting hug, but acted in concert with the Americans and the British like a dragon.

It made sense for the Commission to visit Russia.

'It will be necessary to record,' Justice Mukherjee observed, 'the reasons that prompted the Commission to pay a visit to Russian Federation to search for and collect relevant evidence, if any.'

He goes on to refer to statements supported by affidavits asserting that Netaji related documents existed in various archives of Russian Federation. Witnesses would also be available, it was stated. A major role was played in this regard by Dr. (Ms.) Purabi Roy who claimed to be visiting Russia Federation at regular intervals for research.

Dr Roy gave out the names of individuals who had told her that documents existed in Russian Federation archives which would indubitably prove Netaji's presence there. A list of fifteen archives, where documents relating to Netaji, had been allegedly preserved, was furnished by her.

The Commission's visited Russia from September 20 to September 30, 2005. It visited six archives and examined four witnesses[179] but no concrete finding emerged. There wasn't any record relating to Netaji in five of the six archives the judge visited. A solitary file containing newspaper cuttings relating to Netaji was found in the Russian State Archive of Socio-Political History, Moscow – which was however not relevant.

According to Dr Roy's testimony Russian scholars had informed her about Netaji's presence in their country, and she had provided their names. Justice Mukherjee attempted to meet with these scholars. A couple of such scholars were out of the country. The three scholars the judge managed to meet admitted a long association with Dr Roy, but all of them categorically denied having any knowledge whatsoever of Netaji's presence in Russia!

Prior to the Russia visit, Keshab Bhattercharjee, a lawyer had drawn the attention of the Commission to a passage from a letter dated July 22, 1946 (Exhibit number 228) written by Khurshed Naroji, the grand daughter of DadabhaiNaroji, to Louis Fischer which implied that Netaji was in Russia in July 1946.[180]

"......At heart the Indian army is sympathetic with the Indian National Army. If Bose comes with the help of Russia neither Gandhiji nor the Congress will be able to reason with country".

Justice Mukherjee conceded that the '*genuineness of the above letter*' was beyond dispute. However it was not clear on what basis the lady had made her assertion that Netaji was alive in 1946 and therefore it could not be considered to be anything more than an opinion.

The attention of the Commission was also drawn to a letter dated August 23, 1945 written by Sir F. Mudie (Home Member in the Viceroy's Executive Council) to Sir E. Jenkins (Private Secretary to the Vicery) giving alternative proposals for dealing with Subhash Chandra Bose, *if he returned.*

The argument presented here was that if Netaji had, in fact, died on August 18, 1945 why would the English have been making proposals on what to do in the event that he returned.

There was mild plausibility in such arguments, but nothing concrete.

So nothing came out eventually from the Russia, US or British visits by the Commission.

A report in the Sunday Guardian notes: 'Even the Russian government and the British government did not extend substantial cooperation to the commission, which is not surprising, as the Indian government of the time did not cooperate with Justice Mukherjee. Why would a foreign country give its assistance to an Indian enquiry commission unless it is requested by the Indian government itself ? It is a big question why the BJP did not give complete access to the commission at the time.'[181]

Indian Dragons – Nehru and the Congress?

There is now considerable circumstantial evidence that would tend to suggest that Nehru and subsequent Congress administrations had something to hide, but were they also crouching dragons? The 'dragon' in the metaphor of 'crouching dragon' is a motif for a persona, institution, party or government that commands immense power akin to that of a dragon. Our metaphorical dragon is crouching because it perceives that attempts are being made to uncover a truth, which if successful, will destroy all its power. In Prime Minister Nehru's case we do not know his intentions. Was he motivated by self-interest as is the case with a dragon or were national interests uppermost in his mind? It is clear though that he was willing to do whatever was necessary to stop a certain truth from surfacing.

A side from the surveillance over the course of decades on the Bose family, a matter of public record, the destruction of Netaji-related files, the concealment of non-production before relevant files of files that were not destroyed, there are other circumstances that make the dragon motif appropriate.The air is too full of smoke for there not to be a fire burning some where.

What was the need to put pressure put on Bose's family to acquiesce in the findings by the Committee and subsequently the Commission that Netaji haddied in an air crash?

Nehru's stated rationale behind the appointment of Shah Nawaz at Committee chairperson was never convincing and although discussed briefly in an earlier chapter, it may be worthwhile to discuss it at greater length here.

1. Pressure exerted on Bose's family to accept the plane crash theory

Evidence has surfaced on how even during the time P.V Narasimha Rao was prime minister on behalf of a Congress-led government pressure tactics were employed to get Netaji's relatives to come round to the view that Subhash Bose had died in an air crash. At the time Bose's Austrian wife Emilie and daughter Anita both did not believe that Netaji Bose had died in the plane crash. The following noting is made by the then Home Secretary K Padmanabhaiyah to a file opened on this issue.[182]

'It would therefore be necessary,' he writes, 'to take the members of Netaji's family into confidence in the first place by convincing them as to the genuineness of the ashes. It should then be easier to handle opposition from other quarters like the Forward Bloc.'[183]

The note goes on to say:

'Netaji's wife and the only daughter are at present living in Ausburg, Germany. It is felt that they can best be approached through another nephew of Netaji, Dr Sisir Bose. MrAmia Nath Bose, the most vociferous sceptic of the air crash theory needs to be brought around, by approaching at an appropriately high level.'

What does the expression 'approaching at an appropriately high level' mean? And what does 'needs to be brought around' mean? Persuading someone, not by argument but through inducements could be one way of interpreting such expressions.

Who is Sisir Bose, and why was he willing to try and convince other family members of Netaji's death in the crash?

It turns out that he was a Congress Party member. No surprises here. Sisir Bose became a Congress Party MLA way back in 1987.[184] The Sunday Guardian reports that 'in September 1995,

Sisir Bose's friend who was a powerful Congress leader and a Cabinet Minister at the time personally tried to bring Emilie around the government view.'[185] However she refused to toe the government line up until the end of her life.

Let's examine the wording in that note again. Amia Bose is described by the Home Secretary as the 'most vociferous sceptic of the air crash *theory.*' Is there a Freudian slip here? It appears that even the Secretary is not fully convinced that an air crash took place for otherwise he would have simply written 'air crash' and not 'air crash theory.' And how is Amia Bose to be brought around? Not through arguments, but by 'approaching at an appropriate high level.' Is the tactic here to get Amia Bose to buckle under an approach made by an appropriately high level authority?

The note goes on to assess the probability of getting the family to acquiesce.

'There is good chance that if reasonably approached, the family members may drop their opposition. The question of an appropriate memorial involving the mortal remains shall also have to be addressed in due course.'

'If reasonably approached…' Not through adducing reasons but through an approach that would ask family members who did not believe that Bose ever died in an air crash to 'please be reasonable.' Could it also perhaps mean: Acquiesce – and we will see what favours can be done?

2. Shah Nawaz instead of Justice Radhabinod Pal to chair the Committee

It is said that the former Pakistani Prime Minister Zulfikar Ali Bhutto would not have been sentenced to death had there been one more Sindhi on the judicial bench and one less Punjabi. The death sentence imposed during the time of the dictator Muhammad Zia-ul-Haq was by a narrow majority verdict and a very close affair. All the Punjabi judges came to the conclusion that Bhutto was guilty of the alleged offences and sentenced him to death. It was a split verdict, which went along ethnic lines, with Sindhi judges all voting against the death sentence.[186]

Ethnicity was not an issue in the composition of the first committee that inquired into Bose's alleged death in an alleged air crash, but other concerns were voiced. On the face of things, though, no aspersions could be cast on the selection process.

The Shah Nawaz Committee was a three-member affair. The powers-that-be knew very well that a kangaroo committee would not satisfy anyone. The Chairman of the Committee in particular had to be a person with strong credentials. Who better than a former general of the Indian National Army, someone who actually worked with Bose?

Nowadays the government often uses retired Supreme Court justices for such a prestigious assignment, but at the time the Indian Supreme Court was itself a relatively new institution and there may not have been many retirees among the justices. Anyhow, it would have been difficult to argue that there was anything wrong with appointing a former general with the INA, as the chair of the Committee had it not been for the fact that the very same self-named general was also a member of the Congress Party!

The argument that Nehru's decision to appoint General Shah Nawaz Khan was motivated and disingenuous cannot be easily dismissed. Why? Prime Minister Nehru had not succumbed to pressure easily and had initially opposed the proposal to have a Commission of Inquiry tooth and nail. Given his in transigence and obstinacy, a plan had emerged in West Bengal to have a people's tribunal instead, to be headed by the only Asian judge on the Nuremburg War Tribunal, Justice Radhabinod Pal. It was while this plan was taking shape that Nehru finally withdrew his opposition and agreed to appoint a Commission.

Who was Justice Radhabinod Pal and what was his claim to fame? With his lone dissenting judgement, Justice Pal refusal to become a rubber stamp for the Allied Forces had made him famous in juristic circles around the world.[187] For the Japanese people he was a great hero.[188] Nehru opposed the idea of appointing Justice Radhabinod Pal as the Chairman of the Committee arguing that this might upset the Americans.[189]

The reason he gave was laughable and would insult any reasonable man's intelligence. If Nehru had indeed been so concerned about the feelings of the Americans why did he get India to adopt a pro-Soviet policy? Was that not upsetting to the Americans? The war was over for more than a decade, so it's unlikely in the extreme that this would have upset the Americans. After all, the Commission was to enquire into the death or disappearance of Bose, not into the American role in the war. The enquiry was not related to anything that could conceivably have upset the Americans. Finally, if Prime Minister Nehru was that worried about not upsetting the Americans (and also presumably the English) why on earth would he appoint General Shah Nawaz Khan as the Chairman of the Committee? From the perspective of the Americans and the British General Khan was a war criminal who had even been prosecuted during the famous Red Fort trials? The Americans (and British) would be offended by the appointment of a judge, so this clearly disingenuous argument runs, but not so with the appointment of someone viewed as a war criminal by the British and the Americans?!

In terms of background and experience for the purpose of chairing a Commission of Inquiry, Judge Radhabinod Pal completely outclassed General Shah Nawaz Khan. Shah Nawaz was completely ignorant of the basic rules of evidence and how evidence needs to be carefully sifted, evaluated and assessed. For instance, at one point in the proceedings Chairman Shah Nawaz Khan refused to allow a witness to give testimony with respect to a watch that Netaji wore, with the specious argument that some other witness had already deposed on the subject matter.

Now a Commission needs to weigh the testimony of different witnesses who may make differing statements on the same issue. This witness wished to speak on the watch that Netaji habitually wore, which was different from the one discovered at the site of the crash. It was only through intervention by the other members of the Commission that Shah Nawaz allowed the witness to continue with his testimony.

Was the real reason Nehru and his government did not appoint Judge Pal as the Chair was because they knew him to be of a fiercely independent nature. Judge Pal could not have been persuaded or pressurised by anyone to toe a line. If he had stood up to the might of the Americans and the English, the most powerful governments of the day and victors of the Second World War, it was unlikely that he would succumb to pressure from anyone else! Years of truth seeking and fiercely exercising independence would have come in the way.

Was it the case that a former INA general was chosen because it would look good on paper, but as a soldier, he would more happily follow instructions from the powers-that-be?And yet surely joining the INA itself was a demonstration of extraordinary courage and independent thinking? Critics of Nehru will draw a distinction between those who joined the INA directly and those who were initially Prisoners of War, and joined subsequently. Shah Nawaz belonged to the latter category.

Be that as it may, Shah Nawaz's credentials became questionable because he was a Member of Parliament on behalf of the Congress Party, holding a position of some importance. In that capacity he would surely be unable to go against the High Command within the party were it to wish for him to take a certain position?It was improper for Nehru to have appointed a sitting Member of Parliament, especially keeping in mind the fact that the prime minister had long opposed the setting up of an independent Commission. At the time he was appointed to chair the Committee Shah Nawaz Khan was 'a member of Parliament on behalf of the Congress and Parliamentary Secretary to the Minister of Transport and Railways.'[190] It raises a legitimate question: how independent was this Commission truly?

A second criticism of Shah Nawaz's selection is the allegation that he straddled two independent countries, namely India and

Pakistan with equal ease. The third member of the Shah Nawaz Committee, Subhash's elder brother and author of the 'Dissentient Report' observed with a bitterness that 'even if he does not continue to be a Pakistani, all his relations, including his eldest adult son, and his property are there, and in the course of a comparatively short stay here, he has created a position for himself in government circles and is the proprietor of a mechanised farm with an area of a few hundred acres.'[191] Sarcasm dripping from his pen, he further observes as follows: 'He is one of those fortune favoured persons who has successfully managed to retain his feet on two territories quite profitably. His tact and cleverness in this matter are really praiseworthy. He has been nominated as a representative of Netaji's Azad Hind Government.'[192]

It is unfair to grudge someone his success in the world. After all Shah Nawaz came dangerously close to be hanged by the British for the alleged war crimes that he committed while serving with the INA. It is true however, as Sagari Chhabra points out in her path breaking book *'In Search of Freedom'* that while Nehru favoured a few INA men like Shah Nawaz, the prime minister and the countrywas less than fair, to put it mildly, to scores of INA war veterans, who languished in neglect and poverty. There were those in India who claimed freedom fighter pensions based on a certificate from an Indian Parliamentarian but there were, on the other hand,former INA soldiers in Burma who continued to be stateless![193]

Suresh Basu goes on to assert that Shah Nawaz's actual rank was that of a Colonel, as recorded in secret British Military Intelligence reports, and not that of a Major General which was a title he gave to himself![194]

Shah Nawaz Khan faced trial at the Red Fort for the role he played in the Indian National Army together with General Prem Sehgal and Col Gurbaksh Singh Dhillon. It is a matter of record that he was sentenced to death. That sentence was subsequently reduced to 'cashiering' by the Commander in Chief of the Indian Army.[195]

Generals are there to win battles, not study documents and come to reasoned conclusions, many would say. It's true that had there be an unbiased selection committee Judge Radhabinod Pal would have been chosen – for he was a judge among judges.

With a Congress MP as the chairman of the Commission would people not see that the verdict was sought to be cooked? The government may have been concerned that there could be public protests on how the commission had not been constituted, and such complaints especially those emerging from the State of West Bengal could gain credence.Was it for this reason that the third member of the Committee who was chosen by the government was not a mere member of theextended Bose family, but his real, elder brother?

Reading between the lines of the famous '*The Dissentient Report*' one can easily conclude that the ruling Congress under Nehru suggested to the two other 'committed' members that they try and convince Suresh Chandra Basu to fall in line with their views. Once Suresh Chandra Basu approved the decision of the Committee, not only would the report carry far greater value, it could potentially end, once and for all, the entire controversy surrounding Netaji's death.

As things turned out though, Suresh Basu became a sharp and vocal dissenter. He strongly disagreed with the majority view that there was proof enough to conclusively establish that Netaji had indeed died in the air crash. It was not a quiet dissent. Suresh Babu came out against the majority opinion, all guns blazing!

The government could not have been entirely happy with this verdict. It was true that by majority decision the Committee had concluded that Netaji's death in the air crash stood proved – but there was that lone, but powerful voice of dissent. Were any attempts made to purchase that third vote? Congress spin doctors of the time may have concluded that they could try and get the other two Committee members to persuade and pressure Suresh Basu – but thus far and no further. They would not have had the courage to openly attempt to further influence the third member for fear that such efforts might boomerang on them.

West Bengal at least was not satisfied that the son of their soil had been given justice.

Chapter - 7

Testing the Ashes

I do not attach much importance to my bodily life that I should strive to save it by a process of haggling

Subhash Chandra Bose

Both the Shah Nawaz Committee and the Khosla Commission could not use DNA testing as a method to verify the alleged death of Netaji, because the technology simply did not exist at the time.

In 1986, ten years after the Khosla Commission had tendered its report DNA was first used as an aid in criminal investigation. A British scientist, Professor Jeffereys was the pioneer of this technique and he was still alive at the time of the Mukherjee Commission conducted its enquiry. The inventor of DNA finger printing techniques used them for the first time in connection with two rapes and murders that occurred in 1982 and 1986 in a village in Leicestershire, United Kingdom.[196]

By the time the Mukherjee Commission was established DNA testing had become a well-established technique across the developed world. Justice Mukherjee did not fail to explore the possibility that DNA testing could provide a breakthrough in his investigations.

Visit To Renkoji Temple to Examine the Ashes

The Commission travelled to Tokyo to meet and question Dr.Taneyoshi Yoshimi, the only surviving witness to Netaji's alleged death in a military hospital in Taihoku. Nothing much came out of that meeting. Justice Mukherjee also visited the

Renkoji Temple where the alleged ashes of Netaji have been kept in an urn kept inside a glass chamber. The Chief Priest of the temple was requested by Justice Mukherjee to open the urn to ascertain whether there were any bones in the ashes which could possibly be subjected to DNA testing. The priest regretted that he could not do so, as without a competent mechanic it was not possible to open the glass chamber and for that matter the urn. On that particular date when Justice Mukherjee made his visit (September 16, 2002) it happened to be a holiday, and it was therefore not possible to requisition the services of any mechanic to open the glass chamber and inspect the contents of the urn. The priest assured the Commission that if prior notice was given to him, he would make the necessary arrangement to have the glass chamber and the urn opened.

Since the itinerary of the Commission did not permit Justice Mukherjee to extend its stay in Tokyo, a formal request was made to the Indian Ambassador in Japan to depute a competent representative of his Embassy to inspect the ashes and to report back to the Commission as to whether there were any bones in the ashes.

Was it governmental bureaucratese and red tape that prevented the Commission from delaying its departure by a day on such a vital issue?The Commission had clearly not planned properly to ensure that its time in Tokyo did not overlap with local national holidays. The third Monday of September is traditionally known as Respect for Elders Day, a holiday taken very seriously in Japan with boxes of food prepared for the elderly.[197]

In deference to the Commission's request the Ambassador deputed two senior officers of the Embassy, namely Mr C. Rajasekhar, First Secretary and Mr. T. Armstrong Changsan, Second Secretary to do the needful. Those two officers went to the temple on October 24, 2002 and opened the casket in presence of the Chief Priest and his wife, examined the contents and took photographs. Thereafter, they sent a joint report to the Chairman of the Commission along with the photographs.

What would happen now?

DNA Testing Possible Only on Unburnt Bones

On receipt of the report and the photographs the Commission wrote to the only two institutions in the country at the time that could possibly provide guidance on the best way forward. This was the Centre for Cellular and Molecular Biology (CCMB for short) and the Centre for DNA Fingerprinting and Diagnostics at Hyderabad. A letter dated December 5, 2002, from the Commission enclosed copies of the report and photographs sent by the Indian embassy officials and sought expert advice on whether a DNA test could be conducted on the bones found in the ashes.

The Director, CCMB responded promptly. In his letter dated December 10, 2002 he regretted that it would not be possible to isolate DNA from the burnt ashes, as it would have been completely destroyed.

However if there were any remains of bones (not burnt bones), then DNA presence was likely to be there even if in a degraded form. It could still be used for the purposes of establishing identity. The Director, CCMB further informed the Commission that the special laboratory facility needed for conducting the proposed DNA test was not available in India. The said test could not be carried out in the country.[198]

The Commission was now clearer about the need for unburnt bones for proper DNA testing. Justice Mukherjee understood the issue better now and accordingly requested the Indian Embassy in Japan to get the bones lying at the Renkoji Temple examined afresh,[199] preferably by or in collaboration with an expert and inform the Commission whether the bones seen and photographed were remains of burnt bones or pieces of unburnt bones. In reply, the Embassy in a Fax message dated December 27, 2002 assured the Commission that it would solicit the services of an expert and furnish his opinion to with promptitude.[200]

A DNA expert Dr Heinrich elucidates the situation with respect to genetic fingerprinting as follows[201]:

The identification of severely burnt human remains by genetic fingerprinting is a common task in forensic routine work. In cases of extreme fire impact, only hard tissues (bones, teeth) may be left for DNA analysis. DNA extracted from burnt bone fragments may be highly degraded, making an amplification of genetic markers difficult or even impossible. Furthermore, heavily burnt bones are very prone to contamination with external DNA. We investigated whether authentic DNA profiles can be generated from human bones showing different stages of fire induced destruction (well preserved, semi-burnt, black burnt, blue-grey burnt, blue-grey-white burnt). DNA was extracted from 71 bone fragments derived from 13 individuals. Obtained genetic patterns were compared to the genetic pattern of the respective bodies. Our results show that the identification via DNA analysis is reliably and reproducibly possible from well preserved and semi-burnt bones. In black burnt bones the DNA was highly degraded and in some cases no nuclear DNA was left, leaving mitochondrial DNA analysis as an option. Blue-grey burnt bones lead only sporadically to authentic profiles. The investigation of blue-grey-white burnt bones barely led to reliable results.

In other words, it is not necessary for the bone to be completely unburnt for DNA testing to yield results. Semi-burnt bones can be used successfully; even blue grey bones could 'sporadically lead to authentic results.'

Getting in Touch With Global Experts on DNA Testing

While the matter remained pending with the Embassy the Commission went on with its hunt for an expert who might be able to conduct a successful DNA test on the mortal remains in question. The Director, CCMB recommended a laboratory in Germany where the proposed DNA test could be conducted.[202]

The Commission wrote to Prof. Dr. Svante Paabo, Director, Department of Genetics, Max Planck Institute for Evolutionary

Anthropology, Liepzig, Germany to inquire about the feasibility of a DNA test of the ashes kept in the Renkoji Temple. Dr.Paabo wrote back to express his own inability to perform the work but advised the Commission to contact Prof. Mark Stoneking (contact person: Terry Melton) or Prof. Sir.Alec Jeffreys of the Department of Genetics at the University of Leicester (UK). The Commission redirected his queries to both the experts identified by Dr. Paabo.

The Commission could not have consulted bigger experts in the field. Sir Alec Jeffreys, in particular, was the pioneer of DNA testing in the world – the man who had carried out the very first DNA test in the world, in the context of violent crimes.

Prof. Alec Jeffreys wrote back to express doubt about the success of a DNA test on bone samples which had been subjected to high temperatures and regretted his inability to do the job in his own laboratory. He advised the Commission to contact one of the national forensic service laboratories. Those laboratories, in his opinion, were fully tooled to perform the complex analysis required in the case. The reply received from Terry Melton was on similar lines and he too doubted the success of any DNA testing. According to Melton, cremated remains were very unlikely to give a DNA profile. He agreed to hold a standard forensic mitochondrial DNA test on the ashes including making an attempt to recover degraded DNA, if necessary. He would however only perform the test if recognizable teeth or other anatomically identified parts were available. He recommended a through anthropological evaluation of the remains including photography, and insisted that the anthropologist's report being made available to him prior to his proceeding to do the job.[203]

So the anthropologists report was needed and one of the UK's national forensic laboratories was needed where the test could be conducted. Accordingly, the Commission wrote to the Indian government on January 27,2003[204] requesting it to collect and furnish to the Commission the particulars of the national forensic service laboratories in UK. No reply was received by the Commission.

Any how the first step, the Commission realised, was to have an expert opinion based on a physical examination of the bones present in the ashes. DNA testing would come after. So, it wrote to the Indian Embassy in Tokyo to get such an expert opinion.

The Indian Embassy in Tokyo Makes No Progress

Prompt transmission of an expert opinion was initially assured by the Indian Embassy in Japan earlier, but not furnished despite reminders issued by the Commission from time to time. There were no *malafide*intentions at play here, but the embassy believed that it was for the Commission to choose the names of the experts who would carry out an anthropological evaluation for determining the feasibility of a DNA test yielding any result.[205]

For the Commission to determine who was best suited to conduct those tests in Tokyo, it would have to consult other experts in India. In the meanwhile it appeared from MEA's letter dated May 31, 2004, that the Renkoji Temple authorities had given their assent to DNA test being conducted on the ashes kept in their custody subject to fulfilment to of certain conditions.[206]

Expert advice on the choice of experts sought from the Director, Central Forensic Science Laboratory, Kolkata came quickly via a letter dated April 28, 2004. The Director provided the names and other particulars of three Japanese DNA scientists. Additionally the Director, CCMB, Hyderabad also wrote to the Commission and in his letter dated May 17, 2004 strongly recommended the name of Prof. Saitou Naruya for carrying out the test.

Emboldened by this advice Justice Mukherjee wrote to Prof. Naruya on May 26, 2004, requesting him to let the Commission know whether the DNA test on the ashes in question was feasible and, if feasible, to conduct such test.

In his reply dated June 11, 2004 Prof. Naruya discounted the possibility of a successful DNA test on the ashes in question. In his view DNA examination from such 'ash' is usually impossible because of critical damage to DNA when a dead human body is burned down into ashes. There was only a possibility to compare morphological similarity between some remnant teeth or parts of the skull in the ash with some other reference material.

On June 21, 2004 the Commission again wrote to Prof. Naruya, transmitting to him six photographs of the ashes kept in the RenkoljiTemple and requesting his opinion on whether anything could be done. On July 16, 2004 Prof. Naruya wrote back to the Commission to confirm that it was unlikely that he would be able to extract DNA fragments by using PCR (polymerase chain reaction) from the bones as shown in the pictures for individual identification. At the same time, he wrote to say that he himself was not specialized in forensic science, and if the Commission gave him permission he would get the photos examined by a specialist in forensics. The Commission naturally agreed. However there was no break through.

On July 20, 2004 Prof. Naruya informed the Commission that he had contacted Dr. Yamamoto, a forensic DNA expert of Nagoya University, who had agreed to examine the photos of bones. On July 23, 2004 Dr Nuruyu informed the Commission that after examination of the photos Dr. Yamamoto too had reached the same conclusion. All the bones and teeth shown in the photographs had evidently received tremendous heat. There was practically no possibility to obtain DNA from the bone materials.[207]

CCMB Hyderabad Suggests Sorting out the Bones

Meanwhile modernisation of equipment had taken place in the 'ancient' DNA facility in Hyderabad, brightening the prospect of the proposed DNA test of the ashes. Although the Japanese scientists had given up hope, the Director, CCMB after looking into those photographs was of a different view.

In his letter dated November 3, 2004 addressed to the Commission he wrote that in his view the photographs showed:

(a) the existence of completely burnt bones leaving very little hope for the survival of DNA

(b) but also relatively less charred bones wherefrom it might be possible to isolate DNA for the purpose of establishing the identity of the deceased.

He, therefore, advised that a scientist, specially a molecular biologist, might be requested to sort out the potentially less charred pieces of bones which could be then brought to India in a sealed plastic bag at room temperature.

Obviously, the proposed DNA test of the ashes, if feasible, depended primarily on the access being given by the Renkoji Temple authorities to a scientist for the purpose of collection of the potentially less charred pieces of the bones from the contents of the urn kept in the temple. The question of physical inspection of the ashes by an expert once again came to the surface. The Renkolji Temple authorities were requested to permit an expert to sort out potentially less charred bone pieces from the ashes kept in the urn for the purpose of ascertaining whether DNA could be extracted from it.[208]

The Renkoji Temple authorities turned down the request. In its report, the Commission writes, in dismayed tones, as follows:

Selection of potentially less charred bone pieces from the ashes kept in the Temple without the consent and active co-operation of the Temple authorities being utterly impossible, the Commission, in the interest of DNA testing of the ashes, wrote to MEA again on May 20, 2005, requesting the said Ministry to persuade the Temple authorities to accord their consent to selection of potentially less charred bone pieces from the casket in terms of the Commission's letter dated November 9, 2004 referred to the above so as to facilitate the DNA testing without further loss of time..... [209]

No reply was received either from MEA or the Temple authorities.

The report goes on to say:

From the foregoing it will be evident that so far the DNA testing of the ashes is concerned, the reports received by the

Commission from different experts at home and abroad practically projected a bleak prospect. ***In spite thereof, the Commission, considering the faint possibility of the DNA testing as indicated by CCMB, made persistent efforts to persuade the Temple authorities through MEA to allow physical inspection and collection of potentially less charred bone pieces from the casket lying in the custody….****But on account of the Temple's authorities' reticence as mentioned earlier the Commission could not proceed further in the matter.*

It is extraordinary that the temple authorities should have agreed to DNA testing in the beginning, but later changed its mind even with respect to an examination of the ashes and selection of bone for sending over to India. What would it have mattered if a few pieces of bone were to be extracted?

Why did the MEA take six months to respond? Why did the Japanese temple suddenly turn reticent on the question of selection of bones? After all they appeared to be extremely cooperative when first approached by the Mukherjee Commission. Perhaps the Indian government needed to approach the matter at the highest level.

Till date no progress has been made on this issue. It is true that a DNA test may not yield any results, if there isn't enough uncharred bone available. But at least we could try and then fail? There is simply no excuse for not undertaking this task.

Witness Testimony on the Bones

There is witness testimony on record that could provide some help in understanding what is possibly available inside the urn.

According to the testimony of Mr Nakamura they didn't just take ashes full of completely destroyed bone. They took a bone from each part of the body. Mr Nakamura testified that 'a priest brought chopsticks and as the Colonel (Col Habibur Rahman) could not hold the same, he did so and picked up first the throat bone, then the lower jaw bone, and after that other bones and placed them inside an urn.'[210]

Major Nagatomo, the second Adjutant at the Army Headquarters at Taihoko provides a somewhat different version of events. He confirms that he, Col Rahman and Mr Nakamura went to the crematorium, but then the story is different. He says 'at about 8 am, all three of them came to the crematorium and after unlocking the furnace door that was with him, he pulled out the sliding plate and according to Buddhist custom, he picked up, first the throat bone with a pair of chop sticks and placed it inside a wooden box 8 inch cube, which he had taken with him. He then picked a bone from every portion of the body and placed it in the box. Col Rahman then did the same and after the whole of that box was filled up, the lid was nailed and after wrapping it in white cloth, it was hung from the neck of Col Rahman, and all three of them went in the car to Nishi (West) Honganji Temple for depositing the same there, after due ceremony.'[211]

One could conclude from the testimony that there is the possibility of there being bone fragments in the urn that could be used for the purposes of DNA testing. There are however various contradictions in the testimony of different witnesses that appeared before the Shah Nawaz Commission.

In the first deposition on the ceremonies, it is the priest who deals with the ashes, in the second testimony the priest is missing. There are other discrepancies. For instance there is no agreement on the number of furnaces inside the crematorium. According to star witness Col Rahman there were between 12 to 14 incinerators in two rows[212] but Mr Nakamura states that there was just the one furnace.[213] To add to the confusion and list of discrepancies we have Major Nagatomo saying that there were in all three furnaces or incinerators.[214] Whom to believe and whom to disbelieve?

The entire testimony before the Shah Nawaz Commission is not reliable.

The standard procedure at Japanese funerals involves a fair amount of bone collection, and ninety percent of Japanese are cremated. Large chop sticks or metal picks are used to pick up bones. First the bones of the feet are picked up, and the bones of the head are picked up at the very end. This is to make sure the deceased is not upside down in the urn! The hyoid bone, located in the neck, is one of the most significant bones to be collected.

* * *

After reading up on the subject and consulting with experts, I came to the understanding that a dead person's DNA, if found in the remnants of his bones, can then be matched with surviving relatives of his mother and father – the closer the better. The Bose family is a large clan from both Netaji's mother's as well as father's side, so there should be no problem in getting those DNA samples. The problem was really in recovering, as Justice Mukherjee learnt during the course of his enquiry, proper bone fragment from the ashes kept inside the memorial in Japan. There should have been no problem in sifting through the ashes and seeing if some bone fragments survived and then conducting the tests – but unfortunately that never happened.

There are at least two ways a DNA investigation could be potentially conducted. The first is to see if the ashes belong to Netaji by comparing DNA surviving in the bones with DNA samples taken from his family. The second way, which may be termed the 'exclusion principle', is to rule out the possibility that they belonged to someone of South Asian heritage.

I understand that the East Asian DNA is quite distinct from the South Asian one. If the ashes did not belong to Netaji and to some other person of East Asian descent (Chinese, Korean, Japanese, etc) a DNA test might be able to ascertain that this might be the case. So, through this method we might be able to rule out with a reasonable degree of probability that the ashes belonged to Netaji.

The Bose Family Views on Bringing Back the Ashes

Emilie, Netaji's Austrian wife, since deceased, never ever believed in the plane crash death theory although successive governments attempted to convince her of the same. His daughter Anita was less consistent.

As reported in the Sunday Guardian, a Top-Secret memo[215] for Principal Private Secretary to Prime Minister A B Vajpayee explained how the Indian Ambassador to Germany met Anita on 2 March, 1998 after Emilie had passed away. The memo noted: 'Anita has been to India twice in order to build up a consensus in favour of the return of the ashes, but is clearly uncertain about the results of her efforts.' As a matter of record Vajpayee had taken charge as Prime Minister on 19 March 1998.[216]

The claim made in another top secret 1998 memo is that daughter Anita was now changing her stance and up to the formation of the Mukherjee Commission in 1999 had been supportive of government efforts to bring the Renkoji temple ashes to India and term them as that of Netaji.[217]

The demand for DNA testing was reiterated by Bose's daughter Anita as recently as January, 2016.[218]

"I believe that the plane crash is the most likely cause of his death," Pfaff said when asked whether she believes in the theory that her father died in an air crash near the Taihoku aerodrome in Taipei on August 18, 1945.

However, she said she wants a DNA test of the ashes kept in an urn at a Buddhist temple in Tokyo to ascertain whether the remains belong to the freedom fighter.

"A DNA test could provide proof, provided that the bones are not too badly charred for extracting DNA," Pfaff, the only child of Subhash Bose and Emilie Schenkl, told PTI in an interview from her home in Stadtbergen, Germany.

Is the government listening? It would seem as if the Indian government, especially a Congress led one, would be happy to make the necessary effort to bring back the ashes in their entirety, bones and all, for the purpose of creating a memorial ostensibly to honour Netaji.

It is not however so keen to bring back a sample of less charred bones for the purpose of DNA testing!

The Future of DNA Testing

Technologies for DNA testing continue to evolve every year.[219] Perhaps one day, not too far ahead, the necessity for unburned bones will not be necessary; the ashes will do just as well. A 'chromography' based on an analysis of the ash may yield satisfactory results.

Would A DNA Test Settle the issue Once and For All

Let us assume for a moment that it was possible to do a DNA matching and that a test took place. Let us assume that this hypothetical test showed no match between Bose's DNA (taken from Anita or some other family members) and the DNA present in the ashes. Let us further assume that the DNA test demonstrated that the DNA present in the ashes did not belong to someone of South Asian origin but was more likely to be Japanese. Would this finding conclusively prove that Bose had not died in an air crash? Would all the Bose-died-in-the-air crash people fall silent then?

By no means. Congress Party followers, who are wedded to the Bose-died-in-an-air-crash theory will still not concede the point but suggest instead that there had been a mix up with the ashes. This mix up still could have taken place, it will be argued by their spokesperson, at the crematorium itself where very many people were being cremated or alternatively in transit. Someone else's ashes could have been mixed up in the process of carrying the ashes from Taiwan to Japan. Statistics show that 99 percent of Japanese are cremated, and so, it will be claimed, Bose's ashes could have easily been mixed up with the ashes of someone else, it will be said, since there were others who had died in the same air crash. Supporters of Nehru and the Congress would then argue that merely because the ashes did not appear to be Bose's it *did not necessarily or conclusively prove* that Bose did not die in an air crash at Taipei.

The Road to Taiwan

On the other hand, if it could be proved somehow that there was, in fact, no air crash, it would be evident that Bose had not died in an air crash.

What would Justice Mukherjee discover in Taiwan on the last leg of his travels? Was there any air crash on the date, time and place in question? If there was indeed an air crash was it known who was there on the plane? Was Subhash Bose on the plane? If so, did he survive?

(a) There was no air crash on the date and place in question; and

(b) As a consequence, ipso facto, Bose could not have died in the air crash.

Chapter - 8

A Final Break through at Taipei

A Weak Link is Discovered

It is a challenge for any international conspiracy to keep certain facts hidden from the public. For one thing, it is difficult to keep all the conspirators together over the decades as the motives and situation of individual countries change. Any weak link – and the conspiracy stands exposed.

As it turned out, the weak link that Justice Mukherjee discovered lay in Taiwan. The main witness to any air crash in Taipei would be the Taiwanese people. The extraordinary thing is that their views were never even solicited. Nehru knew even then – that Taiwanese disclosures might upset the so-carefully assembled apple cart – and it was for this reason that he fiercely resisted the idea that the Shah Nawaz Committee visit the site of the alleged crash in Taipei. The Nehru led government might have tightened up secrecy with former colonial power England, and Japan who wished to have good relations with the new Indian government – but the prime minster understood that Taiwan would be difficult to manage. Perhaps, a behind the scenes attempt was made to co-opt the Taiwanese but the Taiwanese government showed independence and did not listen. Who knows?

Nehru prevented the Shah Nawaz government from travelling to Taiwan on the pretext that India did not have friendly relations with Formosa. After India's disastrous war with China in 1962, it was China that could be said to be the enemy, not Taiwan. When

A. B. Vajpayee became prime minister, the government didn't have any surviving excuse to prevent the Mukherjee Commission from visiting Taiwan.

The Justice is Astonished!

Justice Mukherjee must have been astonished to find that the Taiwanese government completely denied that any air crash had taken place on their territory during the specified date. It cannot get clearer or simpler than that. There *was* no air crash.The Taiwanese government not only gave the commission complete access to its files **but even more importantly presented evidence before it that made it clear that no aircraft crash took place in Taiwan on the date in question.**[220]

As the Sunday Guardian succinctly reported:

'The Justice Mukherjee Commission of Inquiry was set up in 1999 to probe the alleged disappearance of Bose. After seven years of probe it reached the conclusion that Bose did not die in the plane crash. The Commission stated clearly and unequivocally that Bose 'is dead but he did not die in the plane crash as alleged; the ashes in the Japanese temple are not that of Netaji.' Curiously enough, the findings were *rejected* by the then Atal Behari Vajpayee led NDA government.[221]

So, at the end of the day, it would not appear to have mattered which government was in power.

The Shah Nawaz Committee was prevented by Nehru from visiting Taiwan. Its successor the Khosla Commission went all the way to Taiwan but thought it unnecessary to meet with the Taiwanese government officials, let alone ask them any questions. Why did Judge Khosla not meet with the Taiwanese? Was it because he knew what he would discover – and did not wish to discover it? Was he acting alone, or at the behest of Prime Minister Indira Gandhi? On her part, did Indira Gandhi know the reason her father blocked the Shah Nawaz Committee from visiting? Was it because that was a three member committee of which one member, Bose's brother, was fiercely independent? Nehru knew that once that Committee arrived in Taiwan, neither he nor the other two members would be able to prevent Suresh Babu from meeting with Taiwanese officials and the man would unearth the truth about the faked air-crash. On the other hand Judge Khosla was Mrs Gandhi's man, so to speak, and he would do what he told to do, and go only where he was asked to go.

These are all really rhetorical questions, and I believe the reader knows the answers by now.

It was finally left to the Mukherjee Commission to visit the offices of the Central Government of Taiwan and well as the local government of Taipei city. It searched for documents which might be relevance and shed some light on its terms of reference. Upon return from Taipei, Justice Mukherjee prepared a memorandum that provided details of documents received by him there and some other documents forwhich a request was made to the concerned official on the eve of the judge's departure.[222]

Justice Mukerjee's Views on the Indian Laws of Evidence

A Commission is not bound by the technical rules of evidence, although Justice GD Khosla appeared to think differently. The Mukherjee Commission on the other hand held that there was sufficient case law from the Supreme Court and the High Courts and the Supreme Court in this regard. A Commission appointed under the Act does not decide any dispute.There are no parties before the Commission, there is no list and the Commission is not a 'Court'[223]

This did not mean that the Commission would ignore the common sense principles that lie behind many of the rules of evidence. It would not be hyper-technical as Courts are sometimes apt to be but at the same time 'to obviate injustice and to demonstrate fair play'[224] the Commission would conform to the cardinal rules relating to reception of evidence. To strike a balance between these two apparently conflicting considerations it was proper to treat any material brought before it as evidence which was'legally probative for a prudent mind' even if it was inadmissible on a strict interpretation of the rules of evidence.[225] At the same time, the Commission would not be justified in relying upon those parts of the testimonies of the witnesses and of the documents which are based solely on hearsay, result of investigation or expressions of opinion (except those of experts) and belief.

According to the Taiwanese There *Was* No Aircrash

When Justice Mukherjee visited Taiwan he was clearly told that there was no such air crash; ipso facto, no air accident related death could possibly have taken place – neither Netaji's nor anyone else's. The Taiwanese authorities confirmed to him during his visit that on the date in question there was no record of any crash at Taihoku.[226] Upon his return to Kolkata Justice M K Mukherjee told newsmen there that the Taiwanese authorities confirmed to him that there was no record of any air crash at Taihoku, the old name of Taipei, between August 14 and September 20, 1945. A precise range of dates had been provided. It was not as if there could be a one or two day error made on the alleged date of the crash.

Veracity of Email Communications Confirmed

Earlier, prior to Justice Mukherjee's visit to Taiwan, journalist and information rights activist Anuj Dhar had already broken the story on how he been in touch with authorities in Taiwan and they had confirmed to him via email that no air crash had taken place in Taiwan on the date in question or within a week before and after the alleged date.

Justice Mukherjee sought to confirm the veracity of those assertions by Mr Dhar. While in Taipei, the Taiwanese authorities confirmed the genuineness of two e-mails sent by Taipei Mayor and Minister of Transportation and Communication to HindustanTimes.com journalist Anuj Dhar, stating that there was no air crash during that period.

"The Mayor of Taipei and the External Affairs Ministry of Taiwan government,' said Justice Mukherjee, 'confirmed to us the e-mails were genuine."[227] There was absolutely no evidence to suggest that any plane carrying Bose had crashed at the old Taipei Airport.

"During the period August 14 to October 25, 1945, no evidence shows that one plane had ever crashed at the old Matsuyama Airport (now Taipei Domestic Airport) carrying Mr Subhas Chandra Bose," Justice Mukherjee said quoting an e-mail sent by Lin Ling-San, Minister of Transportation and Communication, Taiwan government, to the HindustanTimes.com journalist.[228]

The commission was provided with copies of two e-mails reportedly sent by Taiwanese authorities to journalist Dhar. 'The Mayor of Taipei and the External Affairs Ministry of Taiwan government,' stated Justice Mukherjee, 'confirmed to us the e-mails to be genuine.'[229]

The Meticulousness of the Taiwanese

The Taiwanese were clearly meticulous in their research. This is evident from the fact that they do refer to *another* crash a little over a month after the alleged air crash in which Bose died. According to one e-mail from the Taiwanese authorities, there was no air crash during that period while another email makes a reference to a crash on September 20-23, 1945, involving a US C-47 transporter plane carrying 26 people, most of them believed to be former American POWs just released from camps in the Philippines.[230]

That plane, the e-mail said, crashed on Mount Trident in Taitung area, about 200 nautical miles away from Taipei.[231]

No comparisons were carried out between the photographs of that crash that had been placed before the Shah Nawaz Commission with photographs of other crashes in the neighbourhood to show how the photographs of some other crash had been substituted. It was beyond the Commission's mandate to pursue such a line of inquiry. In today's image sharing Internet age such comparisons would take minutes but at the time the technology was several decades away. In the future perhaps someone will discover the real air-crash those photographs submitted to the Shah Nawaz Committee related to.

No News paper Report of any Such Air Crash

It is easy enough to prove that a crash took place, but how does one go about proving that an air crash did NOT take place.

During his visit to Taipei Justice Mukherjee requested officials of the Taipei City Government to furnish the records on the basis of which they gave out that there was no plane crash on August 18, 1945.The Commission was informed that the assertion was based on the fact that there was no report of any such accident in contemporary newspaper accounts kept in their archives.

Taiwan is a rich and developed nation and like other such nations they have enough money to spend on the preservation of records. Newspapers from the period in question were microfilmed, preserved and made available to anyone interested in reading them – unlike the case here, where the Netaji papers have only now been released.

Justice Mukherjee did not take the assertions made by the Taiwanese at face value. He paid a visit to the Institute of Taiwanese History and after a perusal of the microfilmed daily newspapers was able to satisfy himself that there was no report of any plane crash on August 18, 1945.

It can legitimately be inferred that if really there was a plane crash resulting in death of quite a number of persons including Netaji, a prominent and recognized Head of a State and Mr Shidei, a military officer of the rank of General of the Japanese army, the news about the same would have been published in the local daily 'Central Daily News'.[232]

Netaji's Death Could Never have Been Ignored By the Taiwanese Media

The fact of the matter is that, as the Taiwanese government pointed out to demonstrate its thoroughness even news of far lesser importance relating to Netaji's family was published in the same daily ('Central Daily News') in its issue dated September 14, 1945- a few days after the date of the alleged air crash- which, needless to say, indicates that Subhash Chandra Bose was a well-known personality among both the people and the media there. The relevant portion of the said news item, when translated in English, reads as under:-

Central Daily News, 14 September, 1945

*** *** *** ***

The Indian Government decided today to release the younger brother (S) and family of Bose who were detained since the beginning of the Japanese war. The members belonging to the Bose family (clan) who opposed the Government of India will also be set free. The official announcements states, 'In view of the Japanese surrender, there is no need for detaining these people for long time.'

Consider the following scenario. Let us assume, God forbid, that a prominent English politician dies in a road accident in New Delhi. No news of this is published, but a few days later the Times of India publishes a story about his relatively unknown brothers and sisters in England!

Would it not be fair for anyone to conclude in such a case that there was really no accident, and that it was a cock and bull story?

Or take another example. A Bollywood actress, say Deepika Padukone gets married in a public ceremony. Is it credible that such prominent news would not be reported in any Indian newspaper, but a marriage in the Maldives, of her distant cousin, a relatively unknown person is reported?

Is it possible that the Taiwanese media would report on the arrest or release of Bose's family in India, but not report on Bose's death in an air crash in their own country's capital?

Again, how does one prove that a crash never took place short of filming the space twenty four seven? The onus clearly has to be on the people asserting that a crash took place at the date, time and location in question.

The Complete Abscence of Taiwanese Testimony

There is one other factor that appears to have been ignored. Most colonial administrations employ a large number of local staff. Since Nehru blocked the proposal by the Shah Nawaz Commission to visit Taiwan, the only witness testimony that could have been heard at the time would have been that of the Japanese who tied each other in knots contradicting each other's version of the fictitious event that never happened. Had the Commission been allowed to visit Taipei they would not only have had the opportunity to visit the site of the alleged crash, but they would have been able to interview dozens of Taiwanese local staff working at the airfield, hospital and crematorium. No Taiwanese staff is mentioned even in passing by the Japanese witnesses who testified before the Shah Commission. It was almost as if the air crash took place in Japan. If a British general had been badly hurt in any air crash in India, during the colonial period, would not Indians working for the British known about the event, or even possibly attended to him? In terms of numbers, the British were relatively few.

It is not at all credible that with all the Taiwanese staff working in the crematorium, in the hospital and the airfield itself, no word of the crash should have made it to the media. Consider again the fictitious example I have given of a prominent British journalist suffering an accident in New Delhi. Imagine that this news is published in England but not in India. So also, can we believe that the news about Subhash Bose's death was published in Japan but not in Taiwan, the place where the crash allegedly took place?!

Findings of the Calcutta Commission

As stated in its own words the Mukherjee Commission made the following findings:

(a) There is no satisfactory evidence of the plane crash; on the contrary, the story given out in that respect is rather improbable;

(b) In absence of any contemporaneous record in the hospital, the Bureau and/or the crematorium, the oral account of the witnesses of Netaji's death and cremation cannot be relied upon to arrive at a definite finding on the basis thereof; and

(c) A secret plan was contrived to ensure Netaji's safe passage to which Japanese military authority and Habibur Rahman were parties.

Q and A – Conclusions of the Calcutta Commission

The notification appointing the Mukherjee Commission issued on the 14 May 1999 framed five specific questions for it to consider. The questions and the responses of the Commission as published six years later in its report dated 7 November, 2005 are as follows:

(a) Whether Netaji Subhash Chandra Bose is dead or alive
Answer: Netaji Subhash Chandra Bose is dead

(b) If he is dead, whether he died in the plane crush, as alleged.
Answer: He did not die in the plane crash as alleged.

(c) Whether the ashes in the Japanese temple are ashes of Netaji
Answer: The ashes in the Japanese temple are not of Netaji

(d) Whether he has died in any other manner at any other place and, if so, when and how
Answer: In the absence of any clinching evidence an answer cannot be given.

(e) If he is alive, in respect of his where abouts.
Answer: Answer already given in (a) above viz. Netaji Subhash Chandra Bose is dead.

Why Did it Take so Long?

Why did it take so long for us to ask the Taiwanese some simple questions? The Taiwanese would have had no problem in welcoming the Shah Nawaz Committee and offering cooperation. It is doubtful, given the context, that the Chinese would have been annoyed either. It was not the Prime Minister of India who was visiting Taiwan or a state visit of some kind taking place. That could have annoyed the Chinese but not the visit of a Committee investigating a matter of great importance for the Indian nation.

At the governmental level or even with the so-called independent media, no one appeared to care for the truth till recently.

A Piece of Grand Theatre

A little later in this book I have written on how Nehru would have made a great Professor of English. The prime minister was a lover of the arts. He was fond of reading history, literature and poetry. He loved going to the theatre.

Whatever his motives may have been, he actually succeeded in directing a major theatre production in real life even as he fulfilled his considerable duties as prime minister.

That play was titled 'The Death in an Air- crash of Subhash Chandra Bose.' Although an Indian production it received technical assistance from the British and the Japanese. It had a large cast with over a hundred actors, many of them from Japan. It was an ambitious project although the script had its flaws.

'The Mousetrap' a famous English play, based on an Agatha Christie novel, has been running in a British theatre for sixty years, and is considered to be the world's longest running play. The play staged by Nehru has been running for as much time, but people have not noticed.

Perhaps it is now time for the curtain to finally fall.

Chapter - 9

Fanciful disappearance and Death Theories

He asked me whether the statement about the reality of God as against the unreality of the world might not amount to a mere theory. I said, 'It might, but only as long as one simply mouthed it, for the moment it is realised it becomes a living truth of experience, and what is more it can be realised. For those who said so had realised it; therefore we too can follow in their footsteps

(Netaji arguing spiritual philosophy with his father, and later writing of it to a friend)[233]

Where Did he Go?

Justice Mukherjee came to the definitive conclusion that there was no air crash. If we accept this opinion finalized after seven years, as we must, it is clear that Subhash Bose did not die in the air crash. Where did he go then? What happened to him?

Was Netaji Still Alive?

There are various theories about how, where and when Netaji died. Some of them are quite fanciful and even outlandish. There were also parties that appeared before the Commission who insisted that Netaji was still alive!

Justice Mukherjee observed drily that the 'average life span of an Indian is 70-75 year. Subhash Bose was born on January 23, 1897 (a matter of historical record) more than 100 years ago, so it can safely be presumed that be is no more.

Despite the eminent reasonableness of the judge's observation there were Bose lovers, including lawyers who filed statements and affidavits insisting that a person can live beyond the age of 100 years and for this reason Subhash Bose should be presumed to be alive. In support of this somewhat ridiculous claim one such Bose fan attached photographs of a Sadhu aged 124 years found to be living in the year 2000, the year the Commission was seized of the matter.[234]

Different Versions of Netaji's Death

1. Killed at Lal Quila (Red Fort) - a Case of Presumptions and Assumptions

Mr Usha Ranjan Bhattarcharjee, a Calcutta resident filed a statement in which he contended that Netaji was deliberately murdered in the Red Fort in New Delhi on August 15, 1945 at zero hour. Prior to his murder he had been arrested at the Indian National Army's Training Centre in Serambanin Malaysia and brought to Delhi by airplane the previous night via Singapore.

The story was completely without any basis or evidence. Why did Usha Ranjan choose the 15th of August, three days prior to the alleged air crash in Taiwan? Possibly because it made the killing more poignant, since the date coincides with India's Independence Day although India was not yet free at the time.

Why did Priya Ranjan choose the Red Fort as the site for Bose's alleged murder? It makes the story more dramatic considering the Indian National Army (INA) trials that were held there. In the aftermath of the Second World War, many arrests were made by the British of Indians who owed allegiance to the INA. Those arrested overseas were considered to be war criminals and brought back to India to stand trial. The venue for those trials was the Red Fort.

Truth melds into fantasy as far as the prima facie plausibility of this theory is concerned. Why would the British arrest Netaji, fly him to India and then murder him in the Red Fort? There is no evidence that any other INA alleged war criminal was murdered in this fashion. If Netaji were to be murdered as per a British conspiracy – the British did plan to assassinate him in 1941 as per recent revelations – why bother with bringing him back to India and why kill him in the Red Fort?

Perhaps, because having a murder take place in the Red Fort creates a fittingly medieval and mysterious background for this fictitious theory in the mind of its author?

Mr Bhattacharjee did not advance a shred of evidence in support of his theory. It was pure fantasy. He has written a book about the murder but it was really a work of imagination.

According to Bhattacharjee, Netaji was first confined in a secluded cell in the Red Fort. Later he was brought out and shot dead. After this summary execution Netaji's dead body was burnt and the ashes buried in the Red Fort. How kind of the British to follow the Hindu customs in this regard! One would have hoped that he would have led the Commission to the exact spot where the ashes lay buried, but alas, this was not to be the case.

In view of the Calcutta man's persistent assertions he was examined on oath. In the course of his examination he was asked by the Commission if he possessed any proof or document in support of his theory. The man was an author and he promptly produced a copy of his book written in Bengali: '*Netajike Lal Kellai Hotya*' or 'Netaji Murdered at Red Fort.' In the book he described in graphic detail the manner in which Netaji was murdered in the Lal Kella (Red Fort). The judge asked him the source of his knowledge of the murder. The man confessed that, 'the story was given out of presumption and assumption.'[235]

2. Death of A Subhash Bose in A Holy Man's Avatar in 1977

A second version claims that Netaji died at Dehradun in Uttar Pradesh in 1977. We see him assume the garb and mantle of a holy man in this theory. Around the year 1959, the theory posits, a religious center named and styled as the 'Shaulmari Ashram' was established at Falakata in District Cooch Behar, which borders

Bangladesh, Bhutan and Nepal. This Ashram was set up by a Sadhu known as Sharadanandji or Shaulmari Baba to his disciples.

Initially no one took notice of the Ashram or for that matter of the Sadhu. Had it remained a small affair probably no one would have noticed or cared. However when the institute's campus gradually extended its geographical area over 100 acres of land, people started to take notice. The number of its inhabitants also rose to about 1,500 with armed guards posted at the entrance. People in the neighborhood became inquisitive about the real identity of the Sadhu as well as the goings-on at the Ashram.

A few months thereafter, a rumor took root and spread that the man living Ashram was Netaji, in the guise of the Sadhu. This rumor captured the imagination of the common people in the area. The general intelligentsia ignored it in the absence of any real proof that the Sadhu was Netaji. However, the rumor continued to persist and by 1961 it had spread throughout the country.

Intrigued by the rumor, Major Satya Gupta, a former close associate of Netaji, met the Sadhu at the Ashram in February, 1962. Upon his return to Kolkata the Major called a press conference where he asserted that the Sadhu was none other than Netaji. The assertion so made by him was published in different national newspapers on February 13, 1962. Several notable persons visited the Ashram thereafter and met the Sadhu to ascertain whether he was Netaji or not. The issue was also raised in the Indian Parliament and it became the subject matter of a heated debate. The Sadhu reportedly stayed in the Ashram for about six to seven years, but ultimately shifted his location and settled down in Dehradun in 1973. It was there that he died in 1977.

The question whether the Sadhu was Netaji in a disguise came up for consideration before the Khosla Commission. Some persons made strenuous claims that the Sadhu was in fact Netaji; others denied it equally vociferously. This sharp divergence of opinion continued up until the time of the Mukherjee Commission as well. In numerical terms, of the eleven witnesses examined on this score, eight asserted that the Sadhu was none other than Netaji, while the remaining three disputed the claim.

Numbers by themselves however don't necessarily matter. Most witnesses who claimed that the Sadhu was Netaji were only occasional visitors to the Ashram. No reliable document was ever produced in support of their claim.

The only exception in this regard was a Bengali gentleman by the name of Mr Bikesh Chandra Guha. This man produced a letter handed over to him by the Sadhu on October 15, 1967. It authorized him to raise donations on behalf of the Ashram. Mr Guha claimed that the writing was Netaji's. Handwriting experts were tasked by the Mukherjee Commission to carry out a comparison with the admitted handwriting of Netaji, The experts ruled that the author of that letter was not Netaji!

Moreover,Mr Nikhil Chandra Ghatak, a senior lawyer representing the Ashram, categorically stated that the Sadhu had himself denied in no uncertain terms that he was Netaji. He had repeated this denial on numerous occasions in meetings held in the Ashram and outside.

The Mukherjee Commission concluded that: 'there is no reliable evidence to prove that the Sadhu was Netaji.' The question of Bose's death in Dehradun in 1977 did not therefore arise.

3. Netaji Survived A Plane Crash in India– With Hitler

The third theory has Subhash Bose surviving an air crash, but the crash takes place not in faraway Taiwan but in India. As if this were not dramatic enough, Netaji survives the air crash while accompanied by none other than the Fuehrer, Hitler himself. What about Habib ur Rahman who had claimed to be in an air craft with Bose, although that air craft was taking off from Taipei? Geographical details don't seem to matter to the men who float this theory. Habib ur Rahman too was in the same air craft they insist, together with Netaji and Hitler. So…what happened to Netaji, the judge quizzes the proponents of this theory. They too, amazingly enough, have Netaji transforming into a sadhu.

This bizarre theory was propounded byJagannath Prasad Gupta, a resident of village Nagda in the district of Sheopur Kalan (Madhya Pradesh). He asserted that during the days of struggle for freedom of India a plane crash-landed in the neighboring village of Pondola. The three persons who survived the crash were a 'Sadhu', Col. Habibur Rahman and Hitler. Later on, the 'Sadhu' came to their village and started living on the bank of the river near by.

The 'Sadhu' who carried the name of Jyotirdev used to correspond regularly with senior officers in government and used to go out of the village frequently. According to Mr Gupta's assertions, the 'Sadhu' was none other than Netaji and he died on May 21, 1977 in Sheopur Kalan. After his death, so the story goes, the Government of Madya Pradesh had seized all records pertaining to the 'Sadhu' which contain proof of his identity as Netaji.

Three affidavits sworn by Ram Bharosi Sharma of village Nagda, Kartar Singh of village Raipura, and Gurdayal Singh of village Mohana were filed in support of Mr Gupta's statement.

The Commission observed that the theory was 'patently absurd on the face of it and need not be delved into.' Unsurprisingly, the claim that Netaji died at Sheopur Kalan on May 21, 1977 was rejected.

One cannot help wondering if the Commission should have even considered such bizarre, outlandish theories? Why would Subhash Bose, a man who straddled continents in pursuit of freedom for his country, the man known as 'the springing tiger' choose to live the anonymous and reclusive life of a *sadhu*?

Perhaps the better question to ask is: what were the motivations of people who spread such evidently baseless theories? Was the purpose self-publicity or something else?

While attention seeking as a motive cannot be ruled out, we need to remember that there were many people who loved Netaji and wished that somehow their hero be alive! They did not consider how implausible it would be for Netaji to have lived as a *sadhu* in anonymity away from the public eye.

4. Escaped From Russia, Re-invented Himself as Gumnami Baba and Died in Faizabad

The Commission engaged itself in a fairly extensive examination of the fourth theory. The sequence of events described here is as follows: Netaji first escaped to Russia, where he was held in a prison, and then he managed to escape to India, reinvented himself as Gumnami Baba aka Bhagwanji and eventually died in Faizabad.

This theory was examined more carefully by the Commission because here it was not just a few literate and semi-literate witnesses. As many as 31 witnesses claimed that the Baba was in fact Subhash Bose. This included highly educated individuals and senior journalists.

People who had actually met Netaji during his lifetime testified before the Commission that Gumnami Baba was indeed Netaji. Such witnesses included family members such as Bose's niece Lalita who had not only met her uncle Subhash Bose but was familiar with his writing and habits.

This theory that Netaji was Gumnami Baba who died in Faizabad was supported by sworn statements filed by various witnesses. From Gorakhpur there was Dr Alokesh Bagchi. From Faizabad itself there were three witnesses: Mr Ashok Tandon, Mr Shakti Singh andMr Kailash Nath Jaiswal.[236]

The common case made out by them is that after the death of Stalin in March, 1953 Netaji escaped from the then Soviet Union and after coming to India lived at different places in Uttar Pradesh. He was last known to have lived at 'Rambhawan' in Faizabad. Details and particulars of various places where he resided and the duration of his stay there were incorporated in their statements. A further claim made was that in September 1985 Netaji left 'Rambhawan'for an unknown destination. He left behind a large number of household articles including family photos, books, letters and other documents in that house. The custody of these articles was taken by the District Magistrate of Faizabad and kept in the treasury, following an inventory prepared in terms of the direction given in Writ Petition No. 929 of 1986 filed by his (Netaji's) niece Lalita Bose and two others.

Three senior journalists Mr Ashok Tandon, Dr. Viswambharnath Arora, and Mr Sayed Kauser Hussain investigated the mystery surrounding Gumnami Baba and wrote articles in their respective newspapers, magazines and books, relying upon the statements made before them by several persons.[237]Given thatvarious distinguished persons supported the theory that Gumnami Baba was really Netaji in disguise, including Subhash Bose's own family members,the Commission found it necessary to visit Faizabad.[238]

Upon a careful scrutiny of more than 2,600 items lying there the Commission determined than about 700 of them might be relevant for its purposes and brought them over to its office in Kolkata. Writings found in books and journals found in Rambhawan by the said Gumnami Baba were sent for examination and comparison with that of Netaji's by handwriting experts. Teeth too were found and sent for DNA test to ascertain whether they belonged to Netaji's lineage.

Hand writing Analysis

Gumnami Baba's hand writing present in books and journals found in 'Rambhawan' were compared by experts with the admitted handwritings of Netaji. The experts disagreed with each other. While B. Lal, Ex-Government Examiner of Questioned Documents, New Delhi[239] was of the firm opinion that the writings both in Bengali as well as in English belonged to Netaji, other experts held a different opinion. Mr Amar Singh and Mr M. L. Sharma,[240] also in the employment of the Office of the Government Examiner of Questioned Documents, Government of India, Shimla, filed a joint report that the two handwritings belonged to different individuals. Dr. S. K. Mondal of Forensic Science

Laboratory, Government of West Bengal, Kolkata[241]was also of the opinion that the writings belonged to two different persons. Although a dissenting view was expressed, the preponderance of expert opinion seemed to be of the view that the handwriting belonged to different individuals.

Forensic examination of the teeth

Five teeth out of nine were found in 'Rambhawan' that were said to belong to the late Gumnami Baba; the reason for the preservation of so many teeth is not clear. These were sent to the Central Forensic Science Laboratory, Kolkata. The purpose was to extract DNA from three of the selected teeth and compare it with the DNA from samples of blood collected from two descendants on Netaji's father's side and three descendants on his mother's side.

Dr. V.K. Kashyap, a DNA expert and the Director of CFS Laboratory conducted submitted a detailed report concluding that from '*the morphological examination and analysis of SRY gene*' it would appear that the '*forwarded teeth does not belong to either maternal or paternal DNA lineage of Netaji Subhas Chandra Bose.*' It therefore categorically ruled out the possibility that Gumnami Baba was Netaji.[242]

The Commission finally concluded that there was no 'clinching evidence' to prove that Gumnami Baba, also known as Bhagwanji, was really Netaji. The question whether Netaji died in Faizabad on September 16, 1985 did not need to be answered.

Why Did Gumnami Baba Keep Bose Family Photos?

Theories discussed in this chapter are mostly unsubstantiated and can be dismissed outright. The only one theory that is 'relatively' speaking, deserving of some consideration is the Gumnami Baba theory. There does appear to be a physical resemblance to Netaji in the Baba's appearance, to the extent that even family members from Bose's own family were convinced that this was their man. Moreover several Bose related items were found among his personal belongings.

Supporters of the Gumnami-Baba-was-Bose theory continue to insist that this was the case and pointedly ask: how does one explain Bose's family photos, and a drawing of a fighter pilot among Gumnami Baba's effects? Had the photographs been of public events where Bose was present, it would have been possible for someone to get hold of them, but family photos?

The explanation for this may lie in Gumnami Baba being somehow related to Bose, albeit not too closely – for otherwise he would have been identified.

The Bose family was a huge family by modern day standards. Large families were more or less, the order of the day in those times, so to speak, and continue to exist in neighbouring Afghanistan and the tribal areas of Pakistan. If Bose's parents had produced thirteen children, Bose's father himself had numerous brothers and sisters, who also had in turn numerous children. Therefore taken together, with first and second cousins included, we are looking at an extremely large family, a veritable tribe, as it were.

Anyone who has grown up in one of these large extended families will have heard stories of an aunt and uncle who went crazy or simply disappeared unaccountably and were never heard of subsequently. Gumnami Baba was perhaps one such lost uncle who hailed from the extended Bose family.

As someone who himself belonged to the Bose clan, possibly through marriage, he was quite naturally fascinated by the Netaji who was the 'superstar' of the family, if not of Bengal and India itself. The fact that he possessed family photos fits in with this theory. His drawings of the interiors of a fighter jet reflected perhaps his own musings on the alleged death of his illustrious relative in an air crash.

If Gumnami Baba had really been Bose himself there can be no explanation as to why he would not have revealed himself to be the great Indian hero that he undoubtedly was. To suggest that he concealed his identity because he feared for his life is a contemptible suggestion. As the extraordinary life he lived demonstrated, Bose was a man of astounding courage, if nothing else, representing not only Bengal's but India's manhood. To suggest that a man who had the courage to confront the mightiest empire in the world was scared stiff that the Congress Party, or some other villain, would have him assassinated were he to reveal his true identity does not wash. Such speculation insults the man, those who knew him and even perhaps the nation! Were Bose alive and free, as Gumnami Baba undoubtedly was, would he not have wished to meet his wife and daughter?

Rumours about Gumnami Baba being Bose had spread across West Bengal and the country and undoubtedly Bose's wife Emilie and daughter Anita would have heard of them through one of Anita's cousins or uncles. Would they not have taken a flight to India and undertaken a visit to the Baba had there been even a shred of doubt in their minds that this could be him?! No, the whole idea does not make any sense.

Clearly Gumnami Baba was a Bengali with an advanced level of education and sophistication. He had taken up the life of a sadhu for reasons of his own – and yet it would appear that he did not actually wish to live the life of a recluse.

When he realised that some people mistook him to be Subhash Chandra Bose, he was pleased with the error. He knew though that he could not directly stake a claim to be Bose, because then he would be called upon to prove it and under the public glare that would follow any impersonation would fail. But he enjoyed the attention and therefore fed and nurtured the idea that he was Bose without ever stating this explicitly.

The Wish to Believe Netaji Survived the Crash and Became a Sadhu

Of the four theories discussed three prominent theories have him adopt the garb of a holy man or a sadhu. This would appear to tell us more about India and the people who wished to see Bose alive than about Netaji himself. Even when the sadhu himself repeatedly denied being Netaji as was the case with the Shaulmari

Baba people continued to insist that he was Bose and was concealing his true identity for a purpose!

Millions of Indians admired and loved Mahatma Gandhi, but in this vast populous nation of ours, there were also millions, especially among the younger generation who thought of him as an old man with impractical ideas. Gandhi to them was saintly, but boring; Bose on the other hand was younger, dynamic, handsome and dashing. Millions looked to Netaji Bose as an alternative. This was the man they truly admired. While Netaji was a national leader, undoubtedly he was yet a bigger hero in his native Bengal.

The great psychologist Sigmund Freud wrote about how people often believe what they wished to believe. The converse of this is also true: people also try to disbelieve what they do not wish.

When a man such as a Netaji dies, he dashes the hopes and aspirations of so many who looked up to him as their ideal. All these people wished with all their heart that he was still alive. Others were there who wished to say that that he *had* been alive in the new incarnation of Shaulmari Baba, or Gumnami Baba aka Bhagwanji and *they* had met with him and spoken to the great man.

It's a case of 'suspension of disbelief' feeding into the old Hindu idea of a person going into *vanashram* in his later years, cutting himself off from society, in order to understand the true nature of this existence, and contemplate the Divine. The world itself is *maya,* a mere illusion. This also becomes the perfect explanation for why he had not come out into public life.

* * *

During his younger days Subhash Bose was much taken up by the Indian mystic, Vivekanand.[243] In later years he discovered Freud, and unlike Gandhi immediately understood that sexual repression by itself was not something saintly. As the historian Leonard Gordan writes many would like to believe that Subhash never married or that he was celibate and became a spiritual guru in his later years. This fits in, he writes, with the myth building culture in India.[244]

There is of course one other reason why the Sadhu in disguise story fits in so well with Netaji's personal history and life. Aside from his leaning towards spiritual matters since an early age, in his later revolutionary years, Subhash become a master of disguise, when he left Calcutta in 1941, dressing up as a Pathan while traversing Afghanistan and changing his disguise to that of an Italian businessman once he was in Russia.[245] So disguising himself as a Sadhu, in a way, merged both public perceptions of him: as a man with spiritual if not saintly inclinations but also a master of disguise and subterfuge.

Chapter - 10

The Netaji-went-to-Russia Theory

With every blow that she receives in Europe the Imperialist might of Britain is bound to loosen its grip on India....Let us therefore cease talking of saving Britain with the Empire's help or with India's help. India must in this grave crisis think of herself first

Subhash Chandra Bose

Why Would Subhash Bose Go to Russia?

It was the most logical place for Netaji Bose to have gone. Clearly, it would have been impossible for him to have obtained refuge in any of the countries that fought on behalf of the Allied Forces. The Japanese had lost the war and they could not have provided him with any refuge. Hiroshima and Nagasaki had been such a trauma for the Japanese that they could not have ventured to consider the possibility. The Soviet Union was the only real possibility, and the Japanese the only people who could conceivably help him get there.

It will be argued that the Soviets too were allied with the Americans and the British. That may be true, but at the same time, there were fierce ideological differences. It is also a matter of historical record that the Soviet Union was one of the few nations in the world that recognized the INA government.[246]

Some historians have glossed over this fact, and dispute the likelihood that Bose could have made it to the Soviet Union. Their argument is that since the Soviets were allied with the Americans and the British, how could they have considered sheltering Bose

– and how could Bose have imagined that they would do so? On the other hand, perhaps the Soviets understood the subtlety of Bose's position even if many Indian intellectuals, including many of our communists, did not.

The enemy of my enemy is my friend, Bose famously said, but in the Soviet context it was equally clear that for Subhash 'all the friends of my enemies are not necessarily my enemies too.'

Bose's positive view of the Soviets is clear in letters recovered from KGB archives. We find Subhash writing to the Russian Foreign Minister as follows:[247]

Tokyo, the 16th November 1943.

To

His Excellency the Foreign Minister of the USSR.

Your Excellency,

I have the honour to inform Your Excellency that in accordance with the Will of all the freedom - loving Indians in India and abroad - and with the fullest support of all Indians residing in East Asia who number close upon three millions, and of their political organisation, The Indian Independence League as well as with the backing of the Indian National Army now stationed in East Asia - The Provisional Government of Azad Hind (Free India) was established on the 21st of October 1943, with its Headquarters temporarily at Syonan or Singapore.

In communicating this information to Your Excellency, I avail myself of this opportunity to express my sincere desire that there should exist between our two Governments and our two nations the most cordial relations of amity and friendship.

I also take this opportunity of assuring Your Excellency of my warmest esteem. Yours respectfully,

Sd/-

SUBHAS CHANDRA BOSE

Head of the State, Prime Minister & Minister of Foreign Affairs of the Provisional Government of Azad Hind.

Just a little over a year later we find Bose writing to the Russian ambassador seeking the support of the Soviets as follows:[248]

ARZI HUKUMATE AZAD HIND

(Provisional Government of the Independent India)

Hotel Imperial, Tokyo

Monday, November, 20, 1944

To His Excellency Ambassador of the Soviet Union, Tokyo

Your Excellency,

Now, when I am in Tokyo, I would like to use this opportunity to see your Excellency. Looking for this, I put a task in front of myself to find through your Excellency a support of the Soviet Government in the struggle of India for its independence.

2. *The fact, that now we have close connections with Axis powers in our common struggle against British and Americans does not stop me. I am happy to say that Axis powers have a very clear idea about the peculiarity of problem of India and they have kindly recognized the Azad Hind (Independent India) Provisional Government. We are very thankful for it. Besides Japan, whose relationship with the Soviet Union has strictly neutral character, even the Government of Germany has understood in full and appreciated the fact, that we, the Hindu, were interested only in actions against England and America. The Government of Germany also understood and appreciated the fact that we were not interested in the actions against the Soviet Russia. In reality, the activity of my organization in Europe was only against England and America, but not against the Soviet Russia. It was lying in the base of our co-operation with Axis powers in Europe and in this connection we have the full understanding and approval from the side of*

the German Government and Fascist Italian Government.

3. *I know, that there is an alliance between the Soviet Government and Governments of the England and USA now.* ***But I quite well understand the international policy to see that it cannot prevent the Soviet Government from rendering us a support in our struggle for independence. With gratitude I recall the assistance rendered to me by the Soviet Government after I left India in 1941. I conveyed my gratitude for this to his Excellency Mr. Molotov, Minister of External Affairs, in my letter sent from Berlin, which, I hope, was received by him in a proper way.***
4. *During his life Lenin always from the bottom of his heart supported colonial countries in their struggle for independence. It also gives me an impulse. As I know, after Lenin's death the Soviet Government has not changed its policy concerning problems of subjugation of such countries as India at all.*
5. *As far as my party concerned-Progressive bloc, - I can say, that at time when the Soviet foreign policy in Europe was blamed by approximately all parties of India in 1939-1940, we were the only people who openly supported the Soviet foreign policy towards Germany and Finland. What is more, we belong to the left wing of the national movement in India and we have the most progressive views on social and economic problems. Going on, our party is the only one party in India, which up to the present day is carrying on uncompromising struggle against British imperialism in collaboration with some other revolutionary groups.*
6. *I would like very much to see Your Excellency and to find with the help of Your Excellency a support of the Soviet Government in our struggle for independence. As far as the type of assistance, which the Soviet Government can render to us, is concerned, that is such question which should be settled down by the Soviet Government in*

connection with the present military situation. I would like only to add, that we are full of determination to make India absolutely free and those Governments who have recognized the Provisional Government of Independent India unconditionally agree with us in this question. I would like to assure you, Your Excellency, in my highest respect to you and hope to get your response soon.

Still sincerely yours,

Signature
Subhas Chandra Bose

The Soviet Union was clearly aware of Bose's existence and importance. The letter refers to 'assistance rendered to me by the Soviet government after I left India in 1941.' The recognition of the INA by the Soviets would have emboldened Subhash and led him to believe that it held a positive view of him and the struggles of the INA for India's freedom.Besides as the letter itself records, the Soviets had helped him before. Would they not help him again? It is understandable for Bose to be confident that they would. Netaji himself was leftward leaning and he probably understood that it was only a matter of time before the Soviets had a falling out with their war time allies, the Americans and the British because of the different ideologies they represented.[249]

To Russia With Love

There are additional reasons why the Netaji-went-to-Russia theory is likely. Firstly, Netaji himself spoke about his plan to go to the Soviet Union on a number of occasions. Secondly, with the victory of the Allied Forces where else could he have sought refuge? It was the only realistic alternative. Yes, the Soviet Union had been aligned with the US and the English in the World War, but there were stark differences in ideology.

Bose would not have wished to lose himself in some small country. He would wish to go to a country that was large and strong enough not to give him up to his enemies because of some pressure. The Soviets were the one big power that could if necessary stand up to the Americans, the British and the Western alliance in general.

Subhash Bose had considered China as a possibility but that was only before the conclusion of the war. The atomic bombing of Japan had however brought to an end its occupation of China. China was under Japanese control till the end of the WW 2, and Bose's alliance with the Japanese would not have made him welcome there after the end of the war. According to a British intelligence report, previously Netaji had contemplated shifting the nucleus of his government to Yunan province in China and through the communist government there get in touch with Soviet Russia. So Russia had been on Bose's mind for quite some time.[250]

Following the end of the war, Bose quickly settled on Russia, much as Edward Snowden was to do many decades later? Bose would not have inclined to seek refuge in any of the capitalistic countries even had any option existed because of his socialistic views. He was never in favour of capitalism as Patel was; in his mind capitalism and colonialism were too closely linked and interconnected. So, did Netaji make it to Russia and if so how long did he survive there? According to Dr Purabi Roy, who researched Bose's disappearance for twenty years, Khruschev who succeeded Stalin once said that he could produce him (Netaji) within 48 hours if Nehru so wished.[251]

Col Pritam on Why Bose went to Russia Alone?

At least some close confidants within the INA would have known of Netaji's Russia plans. Would he not have felt impelled to take them with him for their security? There are many reliable accounts that now exist about how Netaji always put the interests of his soldiers and followers before his own; in other words he was a true leader. There are extremely moving testimonies of some of the women in the INA which recall that at the time the INA had to retreat from Burma, Netaji refused to leave first and unmindful of his own safety or importance insisted on leaving with the last group[252]. So, the argument runs, since it was uncertain what would be the fate of INA's soldiers arrested by the British, Netaji would have thought of saving a few others in the INA besides himself from arrest and detention and taking them with him to the Soviet Union.

There exists a counter narrative which explains why Netaji could not have taken anyone else with him. Col Pritam Singh, prominent INA officer gave testimony before the Shah Nawaz committee as follows: 'At the Saigon aerodrome, I learnt that the Japanese were of the opinion that it would be difficult to conceal such a big party. The inference I drew from this was that the Japanese wished to take Netaji *alone* to some 'unknown destination.[253]' In his testimony he also stated, 'Netaji told us that the Japanese had informed him that they would like to take him away alone.'[254]

The Manchurian Candidate

The Japanese had surrendered and clearly they would not have wished to annoy the enemy at this stage. It wasn't possible for them therefore to facilitate the departure into Russia of Netaji with a number of his colleagues. They were not even willing to take Netaji into Russia alone, but agreed to take him to a point, Manchuria, from where he would need to make his own arrangements. According to Bose's brother Suresh Basu 'as early as 1944 Netaji foresaw that the Japanese nation would have to surrender and that it was only a question of time.'[255] Suresh Basu records his belief that 'when the time came for the Japanese to surrender, their government expressed great sorrow at the failure of Netaji's mission, and which they ascribed to their defeat, and they then decided to 'respect his last wishes' in whatever manner it was possible for them to do under such changed circumstances[256]. Netaji, accordingly, requested them to take him to Russian territory. This request they could not comply with, because they said, it would embarrass both the Russians and well as themselves, *as they were negotiating for surrender and treaty terms with the Anglo-Americans through the Russians*.

Netaji accepted this, and as a next alternative requested them to take him to Manchuria, which was still under Japanese occupation and he told them that he would make his own arrangements for entering into the adjoining Russian territory. This plan was agreed upon.[257]

The Plan, According to Sa Iyer, Minister in Netaji's Cabinet

Of course if Netaji was to be taken to Manchuria it would all have been done in great secrecy. There would therefore be little likelihood of witnesses that could depose that this has in fact happened. However a number of witnesses testified before the Shah Nawaz Committee that this was indeed the plan.

Mr S A Iyer, at one time a minister in Netaji's cabinet, was one of the prominent witnesses who gave testimony in this regard. In Iyer's view 'the plan was that the Japanese would remove Netaji to a safe zone, so as to prevent his arrest by the Anglo-Americans, who were expected to be in imminent occupation of the territory, and that, after he was safe in Russian territory and out of their clutches, the Japanese would make the announcement regarding Netaji (that he had died).'[258]

The air Crash Hoax Suited the Japanese Too!

Suresh Basu notes that 'as the Japanese were also surrendering to the same Anglo-Americans they could, in my opinion, under no circumstances make an announcement that they had removed alive or had otherwise helped the disappearance of their erstwhile ally, Netaji, who was an arch enemy of the Anglo-Americans and who were naturally very keen on arresting him. So having removed Netaji in a plane from his theatre of activities and away from his countrymen and beyond the control of the Anglo-Americans the Japanese duly announced that Netaji had died as result of the plane crash.'[259]

Every good liar knows that the secret to lying successfully lies (sic) in sticking as close to the truth as possible. Netaji was flying off in a plane to Manchuria. Why not change the destination and create a fiction that he was flying to Taipei instead and fabricate the story of an air crash?

What Would Stalin have Done With Bose?

We concluded in the previous chapter that that air crash in which Bose allegedly died never took place. Bose, the past master of disguise and subterfuge staged his own death in an air crash. It was in the bosom of the Russian bear that he sought refuge with the help of still loyal Japanese friends. How would Stalin have received him and what considerations would have been uppermost in his mind? Given previous communications between the INA and the Soviets, Stalin would have received him well. The consideration uppermost in his mind would have been: how could this possibly benefit the Soviet Union?

Did the British know that Bose had gone to Russia? It is possible that the British came to know through their intelligence that Bose was in Stalin's custody. It is even possible that Stalin himself informed them of this for the world war was only just over and the soon-to-break alliance still stood firm. Nothing prevented the British from raising the issue of Bose's presence in the Soviet Union with Stalin; they were after all war time allies, and the war had only just got over.

It cannot be ruled out that they, the British were even asked by Stalin as a matter of courtesy and formality, for suggestions as to what should be done with Bose. We have to consider that India was still a British colony, and at the time freedom was still an unknown number of years away. In that situation, given that the war had only just ended, Stalin could have consulted only the British (as the colonial masters of India), possibly the Americans, but not the Indian National Congress.

It is true that eventually differences would emerge between the US and the Soviet Union but the Cold War had yet to begin. Most historians would fix 1947 as the commencement of the Cold War and this was still two years away.[260] There are historians who judge that the commencement took place in 1946[261] but that too was a year away. Even if we assume that difficulties had commenced within months of the end of the World War, Bose's disappearance was in the immediate aftermath of the War. Surely Stalin would have consulted with the British and the Americans.

What Would the British have Wished Stalin to Do With Bose?

At the highest levels of the British establishment, after reviewing the post-war situation in India – the grounds well of public anger against the arrests and planned hangings of INA patriots they (and possibly, the opportunists within the Congress) would not have wished for Bose to return to India **under any circumstances** be it as a prisoner of war or as a free man.

It is possible even that the British asked Stalin to

(a) Hand Bose over to them (most preferred option)

(b) Have Bose executed secretly, without letting the world know (second best option).

(c) Keep Bose incarcerated without disclosure

Bose's release would have been terribly inconvenient for the British from both a short term and a long term perspective. If Bose returned to face trial, he would become a rallying point for millions of Indians and the demand for immediate grant of independence in the short term. At the same time, taking a longer view of matters, were Bose to return and then take center stage in Indian politics, which was more than likely, their own relations with India, would undoubtedly suffer as a consequence.

Many people may raise their eyebrows at the suggestion that the British could have conceivably asked Stalin to get 'rid' of Bose, but this is far from being an outrageous suggestion. As a matter of fact the British made several attempts to assassinate Bose. There was a war going on, a world war at that, and Bose was a thorn in the British backside. British historians have researched this issue.

The British Plot to Assassinate Bose in 1941

Eunan O' Halpin is a historian at Trinity College, Dublin. The author of a number of books on British intelligence he writes about a plot by the British to assassinate Subhash Bose in 1941 that was formed soon after Bose fled Calcutta for Germany.[262] The British took Bose very seriously, and Halpin writes that clear instructions were issued. O'Halpin based his report on British intelligence documents declassified only a decade or so previously in 2005[263] now a matter of public record.

Conspiracy theorists use this evidence of plotting to assassinate as corroborative proof that the Brits did actually get Stalin to kill Bose. It is not a completely outlandish or unreasonable theory. On the other hand, others argue that while the Britishwanted Bose dead in 1941 at the outset of the Second World War, they would not have thought it necessary in 1945 **when the battle had been won!** Was there a good reason to kill Bose in 1945? Could henot have been tried together with the 200 other INA prisoners (although these trials were eventually abandoned)?

It is not difficult to understand that the British wanted Bose to be dead at the outset of the war. If Bose's logic was clear enough – the enemy of my enemy is my friend, for the British, when they plotted to have him assassinated the reverse logic was likewise obvious – the friend of my enemy is my enemy.

Bose's Indian National Army had two main sources of recruitment. Firstly, there were the Indian prisoners of war (POW's) who were fighting on behalf of the British but had been captured by the Japanese. Many had already received training on the battlefront at the hands of the British. These were Indians who had been taken as Prisoner of Wars by the Axis powers. It was a stroke of genius to enlist them in the INA, a win win situation. No matter how badly POW's are treated, they still represent a drain on a state's resources. By investing a little bit more if these POW's could somehow be reprogrammed as a result of Bose's leadership to see that they had mistakenly been fighting for the enemy (the British) instead of against them, it would be a boon for the Japanese. The POW's too would be happy, for now they would be treated with respect, as 'true' freedom fighters, rather than British mercenaries. It would not have been very difficult to convince them of the clear logic that Bose propagated – why risk your life fighting for the British who weren't even willing to offer you independence if and when the battle was won?

Secondly, there were millions Indians living as minorities in Singapore, Malaysia and Burma who swelled the ranks of the INA. The INA could not carry out a major recruitment exercise from within mainland India itself where the nationalist politics and struggle was largely under the control of the Congress and Gandhi. For the British, in that sense, it suited them to have Gandhi, the man of non-violence in charge. At the same time, although the number of Indians joining Bose's INA from mainland India itself might have been numerically small, they could soon take on a life of their own. What started off as a trickle might overtime turn into a stream and then that stream might turn into a flood.

Worse still, Bose's plan could spark similar movements in other colonies across the British Empire. It was not that Bose's formulation was entirely unique; there may have been instances of other groups within other colonized nations also planning on aligning with the Axis powers. India however held a special importance in the overall scheme of things and the far-seeing British saw that what Bose was doing could indeed be very detrimental to their interests.

Why Stalin would not have Released Bose

On his part, Stalin would have seen no advantage in releasing Bose to the British. The man was after all a freedom fighter, fighting against the evils of colonialism and capitalism, more or less a fellow comrade-in-arms.

Bose was too valuable a bargaining chip for Stalin. The Soviet would not have been so hasty as to kill this golden goose, or hand it over to the British.

It is conceivable that Stalin may have told Bose that it wasn't the right time to announce to the world that he, Bose, was still alive. It was also not the right time to release him secretly – where would Bose go? If he made his way back to India, he would almost certainly be killed by the British. As a consequence I believe that it is likely that Bose was kept in 'protective custody' even as Stalin watched future developments in India.

While in Soviet custody, Bose would have been kept in very good condition, with all manner of comfort and medical and other facilities being provided, somewhat like a VIP – although in a high security environment (the KGB had a complete dossier on him and knew of his various escapes). Periodically, say every three months or so, progress reports would be sent to Stalin.

But a further question surfaces: if Bose was indeed in 'protective custody' why would Stalin have not released Bose in 1947 when India attained independence? After all Stalin remained in power for six years after Indian independence, dying only in 1953.

We will answer this question in the next chapter.

Chapter - 11

What Nehru Knew

Though there may be no immediate tangible gain, no sacrifice is ever futile. It is through suffering and sacrifice alone that a cause can flourish and prosper, and in every age and clime the eternal law prevails – the blood of the martyr is the seed of the church

Subhash Chandra Bose

Character is Destiny

Character is destiny, they say. Great novelists and playwrights often understand character better than say, historians, journalists or intellectuals. Journalists and historians will try and track down documents that prove what happened to Bose, and if they do not find anything, throw up their hands in despair and simply give up. This creates space for some people to spin yarns and impossible tales, and unfortunately such people do not appreciate how Bose's character was at odds with the reclusive *sadhu* he was supposed to have become.

You could say that some such thing happened with respect to Bose. There were those who thought he was a *sadhu*, named Jyotirdev, who survived an air crash with Hitler of all people. Others came to the conclusion that he was Shaulmari Baba who died in 1977.

Yet others swore that he was none other than Gumnami Baba. Journalists, intellectuals and even Bose's relatives (which included a sister) were convinced that Gumnami Baba was none other than Bose in disguise. 'Fifteen lakhs of people should have attended the funeral,' writes journalist Anuj Dhar on Gumnami Baba's funeral,[264] 'but only a few hundred did.'

Millions of people preferred to believe that Bose died in peace as an enlightened *sadhu,*rather than in an air crash or under 'protective custody' in the Soviet Union. This is a happier, feel-good ending in some ways, but it can be believed by only by someone who either does not understand Bose's character, or prefers to ignore it.

If you were to ask those who insist that Bose died as a *sadhu* in India, why on earth the man did not come out in the open, the standard reply given by way of explanation is that Bose feared for his life. Our hero was worried that Nehru or the Congress would send someone out to assassinate him. In Gumnami Baba's case, relatives, journalists and other important people in the believers club pointed to various 'proofs' that 'conclusively' demonstrated that the Baba was none other than Bose himself.

All these relatives, journalists and important people needed to ask each other a simple question: was this morbid fear of assassination in line with Bose's character? Anyone who understood Bose's character would have dismissed such theories outright. Bose, the freedom fighter, the warrior, a man who straddled continents in dogged pursuit of freedom for India, the man known as the 'springing tiger' – would such a man fear for his life, and that too from an Indian government? Impossible! Living the life of a fearful saint would have been so much out of character, that the hypothesis should have been simply dismissed out of hand without any further consideration. In this sense, chapter 9 of this book ought never to have been written.

An Analysis of Nehru's Character

Bose's character tells us that he could not have become a holy man in hiding, but it cannot alas tell us what happened to him. On the other hand Nehru's character taken in conjunction with his behaviour can lead us to conclusions on what happened to Bose.

In order for this to happen, Nehru's character has to be understood and carefully analysed. An assessment can be made thereafter of what India's first prime minister would have done and what he would definitely not have done in relation to his former colleague, Subhash Bose. This is not a book on Nehru so the following portrayal and assessment of his character will necessarily have to be confined to a few pages.

Aristocratic and over-anglicized

Nehru's was a flawed character, but aren't we all flawed? The former prime minister's leadership and judgement too was often flawed, which is a more substantial and serious charge, since it had inimical consequences for India. Aristocratic and over-anglicised, he himself wryly admitted once that he was the last English ruler of India.

Jawaharlal was English in his accent and in very many of his thought process. An admirer of British institutions and democracy he was nonetheless not above nepotism and favouritism. His promotion of his daughter Indira Gandhi, and insistence that his sister Vijayalakshmi Pandit become the first Indian Ambassador to the United Nations are two such examples.

Misplaced idealism and flawed decision making

Nehru's blunders were, paradoxically enough, often caused by his impractical idealism and high moral posturing, something he may have imbibed from the mahatma.

Nehru, for instance, was completely opposed to India having a nuclear bomb. The writer Arundhati Roy would have found a soul mate in him in this regard. He actually*declined* the US President's offer to help India build a nuclear bomb before China, once it was clear that the Chinese were determined to do so.[265] A recent biography by a former diplomat refers to this consequential decision.[266] It could be legitimately argued that this had major, unfortunate consequences for India and its security – but the decision itself was prompted by a flawed idealism and naiveté.

Nehru critics will point out that if India had taken US assistance and exploded a nuclear device, the 1962 war with China may never have happened. Not only the 1962 war but the 1965 war with Pakistan would never have happened.

With the same misguided idealism Nehru as India's first prime minister rejected Maharaja Hari Singh's offer to join India *until and unless the Raja complied with certain, clearly untenable decisions.* The current problems in Kashmir would not have existed had Nehru shown greater sagacity.

Finally we may take the case of the belated inclusion of Goa within the Indian union. When the British left, they left behind a huge Indian army and military hardware. This was not an act of generosity on their part, but it was simply not economical to transport everything back to England. Given the strength of the Indian army and the hardware it possessed the Portuguese could not have kept Goa by force. Sardar Patel was famously quoted as saying that getting rid of the Portuguese should be a 'two hour' job. However Nehru didn't want to upset the Portuguese and preferred to wait. As a consequence,Goan independence from the Portuguese was delayed by fourteen years.

The point in making all the above references is to show that Nehru made several immature and irresponsible decisions but these were prompted by high, if flawed idealism.

A poetic temperament

Nehru was poetic, a dreamer, and hated violence. Gandhi too hated violence and transmitted this part of his philosophy to Nehru but he was neither poetic nor a dreamer nor an aesthete. But Nehru hated violence on his own; it may have one of the reasons he was drawn to the *mahatma.*

A socialist at heart, Nehru hated the word 'profit' and considered it to be a dirty word. He was no fan of the private sector.

Nehru died with a book of poetry on his desk opened on a page that contained Robert Frost's famous verses -*The woods are narrow dark and deep, but I have promises to keep*....This poetic side to his personality and the good looks he was gifted with made him a lady-killer.

An Ambitious Man

High morality and idealism co-existed with fierce ambition in Nehru's persona.The evidence of Nehru's naked ambition is there in his fierce lobbying for the prime minister's post. He made it clear that he was not willing to play second fiddle to Sardar Patel (whereas the latter was willing to be number two in the national interest). Gandhi indulged Nehru's unwillingness to accept anything but the top job and anointed him as his favourite. Nehru knew that he did not command much support in the Provincial Congress Committee's relative to Patel, but ambition spurred him on. It was all or nothing for Jawaharlal and he succeeded in emotionally blackmailing Gandhi.

In later years, after the Chinese debacle in 1962, he should have in all fairness resigned, but chose to stick on to his position. An enquiry into the reasons for our terrible performance in the war with China was inevitable, but Nehru tried his best to scuttle it, and when that was not possible blocked public disclosure of the report. The Henderson Brooks-Bhagat Report on our failings in the 1962 war has not been made public till now.

Was Nehru's idealism faked or put on?

Nehru haters believe that the professed idealism was false and a charade but the evidence does not support their case. This was a man who made great sacrifices for the nation spending many years in jail separated from his wife and daughter. A learned person, he wrote informative and reflective books even if he never completed a truly outstanding or great work of history.

At the core Nehru was a tender-hearted man. Some may say that Gandhi had communicated his idea of non-violence to him effectively but it was probably in his very nature to begin with. For this reason he neglected the development of military infrastructure and the Indian armed forces. An intellectual and orator, he was, at the same time, in many ways an impractical man who should not perhaps have been running the country. He may have been more suited to the position of a Professor of English Literature or History or to an ambassadorial position. Although he considered himself to a history buff he often chose to ignore real-politic considerations that ought to have informed important foreign policy decisions.

So, that in a nutshell is my Nehru. Now for the questions that need to be answered with respect to Bose's disappearance, keeping such a personality and character in mind.

The Q and A Reading From an Analysis of Nehru's Personality

In this last chapter I propose to approach the question about what happened to Bose from a different angle than has been previously attempted. This is an essentially subjective approach of what, in my opinion, Nehru knew about Bose's disappearance and death. Nehru's behaviour suggests to me, for instance that *even he* wasn't one hundred per cent certain about what happened to his erstwhile colleague.

1. Did Nehru Know More than he Let on with Respect to the Bose Saga?

The answer to this question is an unequivocal and resounding 'Yes!' Nehru certainly knew more than he let on. It explains his great reluctance for there to be a public inquiry into Bose's disappearance as also his stubborn insistence that Bose was dead, having died in the alleged air crash that happened in Taipei. Not only did he know more than he let on, he knew perfectly well that there had been no air crash in Taipei. It was for this reason that he forbade the Shah Nawaz Commission from travelling to Taiwan on the specious ground that this could affect relations with China.

2. Did Nehru have Something to Hide?

It is also clear now with the benefit of hindsight that Nehru and the Congress government was hiding something. It was moreover not something inconsequential that he was hiding, but a powerful secret the disclosure of which would have major international consequences. The question really should be: was Nehru hiding things in general public interest *or in his own interest.* We will attempt to answer this question just a little ahead but there can be little doubt that Nehru had things to hide, whatever may have been his motivations.

This wasn't the case of an odd misplaced file, where it may have been possible to give the government the benefit of the doubt. There were hundreds of files on Bose that were available that should have been made available to the committee and commissions that inquired into his death or disappearance. Nehru himself could not have been ignorant of the existence of all these Netaji related files, but deliberately played dumb.

One question that arises is: why weren't at least a few files made available to the Shah Nawaz Committee for forms sake, if nothing else? Most if not all material within was in any case harmless. There can be only one explanation: the prime minister's paranoia. Just to be on the very safe side, it was decided not to give any file at all. The stakes for the Nehru were simply too high. Who knows how some wrong paper might get inserted into a file?

3. Was Nehru Worried about Revelations Concerning Bose Coming to the Surface?

Yes, without any doubt Nehru was extremely worried revelations concerning Bose could come to the surface. One of the main fears that played in his mind was that the truth would somehow become known that there had been no air crash in Taipei – and therefore Bose could not conceivably have died there.

Once this truth was known there would automatically be a powerful seed of doubt planted in the public's mind: had Nehru known that there was no air crash all the while? The public would then ask a further question: what else had Nehru known?Even if he pleaded ignorance, the doubt would persist, and there would be enormous pressure on the prime minister to uncover the entire truth and disclose it to the public.

What is the basis on which can we conclude that Nehru was worried about certain revelations coming to the surface? Two things confirm Nehru's fears. Firstly, as already stated, the intriguing fact that hundreds of files existed in central government archives but these were never made available to the Shah Nawaz Committee. What was the purpose behind secreting these files away from the scrutiny of the Committee if it was not fear of certain revelations? Secondly, not only did the government not produce Bose related files before the Committee, ostensibly under Nehru's instructions, it was also worried that some information concerning Bose could come via the post and therefore ordered the interception of all mail to his relatives in Calcutta. It is now a matter of historical record that the Jawaharlal Nehru government spied on the relatives of Subhash Chandra Bose for nearly two decades. It is clear that this was not accidental but a deliberate act on the part of the government. The spying wasn't confined to *watching* the activities of the Bose family. As reported in the press, Intelligence Bureau (IB) 'sleuths intercepted and copied letters written by the Bose family *and even trailed them on foreign tours.*'[267]

When the facts around this existence of this extensive and prolonged surveillance came to light, the family members of Bose and lovers of Netaji took out a rally condemning the snooping carried out by successive Congress governments. The rally was attended by over a hundred people.[268]

The question arises: was Nehru worried for himself, and his own political future? Or was it the case that he was genuinely worried for India's relations with certain countries, notably Russia and the UK were some facts come to light. What were those facts?

4. Did Nehru Feel 'Guilty' about Something?

Nehru knew that there had been no air crash in Taipei. He also knew that Bose had therefore never died in the air crash. He felt guilty for hiding this information from the general public, even though he hid this information based on his perception of where Indian interests lay.

Nehru kept Bose's family under surveillance for decades. The fear that the truth about Bose would somehow come to light haunted him so much that he even set the Indian Embassy to spy on Bose's nephew while he was travelling in Japan.

Tailing the Bose family and intercepting their mail was one thing but information has now leaked that Nehru asked for a report as to whether a nephew of Bose had visited the Renkoji temple where Bose's ashes were stored. Journalist Swapan Dasgupta naively considers that a possibility could have been that 'Nehru's curiosity could well have been genuine and not governed by anything sinister.'[269] Curiosity? Yes, but what about? Curiosity about whether a certain nephew revered his uncle sufficiently to have visited the shrine where his ashes were kept? Or was it concern and fear that the nephew would somehow discover the truth that the ashes kept in the temple did not belong to his uncle Subhash Bose? Why would Nehru even bother with the movements of a stray Bose nephew in Japan? Come to think of it, why should Nehru even be *aware* that a Bose nephew was visiting Japan? Ah, but they had mounted that surveillance on the Bose family. So much for Harvard professor and Nehru apologist Sugata Bose's argument that that in the absence of conclusive proof that Nehru ordered surveillance he would be inclined to give him the benefit of the doubt. If Nehru went to so far as to enquire as to whether the Bose nephew went to the Temple, he had certainly something to hide – a terrible, dark secret.

No, the argument that it was innocent and idle curiosity doesn't really wash. If it were an ex-lover one could be interested in knowing his or her movements. A nephew?! Not even Bose's wife or daughter – that at least could have been remotely if not properly credible.

If Nehru knew that Bose never died in an air crash did he also know where it was that Bose went?

Let me go a step further here now. Yes, Nehru knew very well that Subhash had gone to the Soviet Union via Manchuria and had thereafter met with the Soviet leadership.

Nehru concealed this information from the Indian public. He felt guilty for concealing both these important pieces of information, and he also worried what the consequences would be for him, were the truth to surface.

This was the real reason the Intelligence Bureau had been intercepting all letters to the Bose family for decades? The government of the day was worried about the possibility of a letter being smuggled out of the Soviet Union by Bose or someone known to him revealing how Subhash Bose had entered the Soviet Union and met with the top Soviet leadership. That revelation would really have set the cat among the pigeons, as the English expression goes.

5. Did Nehru Benefit in any Way From Bose's Disappearance?

Bose's appearance in India would have certainly been inconvenient for Nehru for his position as prime minister would have immediately come under threat and his own image building exercise would have come to a halt. The *numerouno* in Indian politics was Mahatma Gandhi and Nehru became prime minister courtesy Gandhi the king maker who asked an unhappy but obedient Sardar Patel to step aside and make room for his blue-eyed Kashmiri boy. Unlike Nehru, widely seen as Gandhi's protégé, Bose had an independent stature, position and claim to the crown.

The benefit was clearly there. This is the reason why Bose lovers and Nehru haters put forward the argument that Nehru conspired with Stalin to keep Bose in custody till he eventually died.

Nehru may have genuinely believed that the release of Subhash soon after independence would muddy the waters for his leadership to oversee the peaceful transition to socialism. Subhash' s release, he may have worried, could possibly destabilise newly independent India's relations with the British, which was not the best thing to happen – given the effort he and Gandhi had put into making sure that this did not happen.

Nehru may well have benefited politically from Subhash Bose's disappearance, but this was happen stance, and did not mean that he personally did anything to make sure that Bose did not reappear.

6. Did Nehru ask Stalin to Have Bose Executed?

Nehru may have been ambitious but he was not an evil man. Both Bose and Nehru had been Presidents of the Indian National Congress prior to independence, unlike the Father of the Nation Gandhi, who thought factories were evil, they shared similar ideas about the importance of industrialisation, (even though Nehru broached his differences with the Mahatma much more delicately) and they were both in prison for the cause of Indian independence. Nehru could not have faced himself if he had indeed ordered Bose's execution as is alleged by some supporters of Netaji. Nehru's nature was simply too soft to be a murderer. His idealism was often flawed and misplaced but it would never have permitted him to order or request an assassination.

7. Did Nehru ask Stalin to Keep Bose in Custody?

Again, not possible. I am far from being a Nehru hater or baiter. In my understanding of Nehru's character, I cannot believe that he could have ever (a) asked Stalin to keep Bose confined in prison and (b) asked Stalin to have him executed, so that there would be no danger to his position as prime minister were Bose to someone magically resurface.

8. What Secret was Nehru Hiding? was It That Bose had Died in the Soviet Union?

The answer to this question has to be – YES. This indeed was the terrible secret that Nehru nursed in his bosom. Having faked his death in the air crash that never happened, Bose had headed off to the Soviet Union. He had been well received by the leadership, but kept in custody, albeit of a VIP variety, and had died while still in Soviet custody.

Once India became free, and Nehru became prime minister, the Soviets got in touch with him and told him that Bose had died while he was in their custody. Did Nehru wish for Subhash Bose's remains and possessions to be shipped to India?

Nehru was both shocked and saddened at hearing the news. He wished greatly for India to be friends with the Soviet Union and to be closer to them than to the United States. According to his thinking and the socialist ideology he was drawn to, India would follow a socialist path. He was not over-fond of free enterprise and disliked the word 'profit'.

After careful consideration he informed the Soviets that perhaps it was best for them to remain quiet on the issue. There was no question of their sending the remains of his body and his last possessions or writings (if they existed) back to India. No purpose would be served if it was disclosed that Bose spent his last years in the Soviet Union. Nehru knew his people well enough. Indians were emotional people, and would surely demand to know why this had not been disclosed by the Soviets earlier, if they claimed to be India's friend. Future relations between India and the Soviet Union would be endangered. There would be suspicions that the Soviets had first kept Bose in custody and thereafter had him executed at the behest of the United Kingdom, and this would be an allegation that could have been difficult to definitively refute. After all, the Soviets had been aligned with the British and the Americans in the World War, and it had taken some time before their differences sharpened. It could be reasonably argued that the Soviets had consulted with the British, the British has suggested extermination of Bose, and Stalin had obliged. India had only just gained freedom and independence, Nehru reflected, and if its relations with two of the great powers of the day were somehow endangered, it would not augur well for the country and its future.

9. Did Nehru Become Unsure Later If Bose had Really Died in the Soviet Union?

In the beginning trusting Nehru believed the Soviets one

hundred percent that Bose had unfortunately died while he had been in their custody. However, as the years passed, he became less and less sure of this. After all, he began to think, neither he nor anyone else had actually ever seen Bose's dead body. Yes, it was true that the Soviets had offered to send Subhash's remains to India but perhaps they were bluffing? Perhaps Bose was still alive and in their custody and they planned on using him as a secret weapon should the need arise. The Soviets were happy enough with Nehru and his socialist views. They did not see that any special advantage would accrue to them were they to release Bose and send him back to India.

If Nehru strayed too far from the Soviet line, they would threaten to expose him. Perhaps this real or imagined fear had made Nehru jittery?

Whatever it was, Nehru's faith in the Soviets was no longer as rock solid as it had once been. And since he had not actually seen Bose dead, but only had the Soviet's word for it, he could not be sure. Perhaps the Soviets had sent him photographs of a dead Bose, but Nehru, with his behind-the-scenes oversight of the Shah Nawaz Committee, knew better than most how such photographs could be easily doctored.

10. Had Bose Really Died or had the Soviets Bluffed?

Let me outline three possible scenarios for the reader and then give my own impression of where the truth lies.

The first scenario: Stalin knew there were no guarantees that India would continue with its socialist policies that made it closer to the USSR than to the US. The Russian leader was alert to the fickleness of political alignments, and so Stalin kept Bose alive in a kind of VIP 'protective custody' instead of 'purging him' as the socialist dictator did with hundreds of thousands of others. Bose was alive but Stalin told Nehru that he was dead. Keeping Bose alive (and also well fed) was also one way of ensuring that Nehru (and India) did not stray too far from the Soviet bloc and way of thinking. If Nehru were to steer India away from the socialist model, the Soviets would at once have Subhash Bose released unleashing turmoil within the nation, and a call to return to socialist values. It never ever came to that as things developed. Nehru was a genuine socialist in any case, but of course he could not have afforded to have Bose released and return.

The second scenario: Bose had actually died while in Soviet custody, but the Soviets knew that Nehru could not be one hundred percent sure of his death. So they toyed with him and later his daughter Indira keeping them and India on the straight and narrow socialist path.

The third scenario: Bose had actually died, just as the Soviet's had told Nehru. There was never any deviousness on their part in this regard. Theyvalued their relationship with India too much to ever play games with Nehru or threaten him in any way. It was Nehru's own feelings of guilt that created the problem. He felt guilty that he had told his people the truth, and brought Bose's remains, possessions and last writings home to India as the Soviets had offered, and accorded him the respect he so richly deserved.

This guilt troubled him deeply. It was the real reason that Bose's portrait never adorned the central halls of the Indian Parliament. Nehru's decision to keep Bose's death in the Soviet Union hidden had been a momentous one and it weighed on him enormously. He had the case of the nerves on anything concerning Bose. He may have pondered on the question whether the Soviets had 'played' him, and may have imagined that some of their acts were in the nature of threats, and that there was a possibility that Bose could suddenly turn up alive. But it was really all in his head.

For myself, although absolute certainty is not possible on which of the aforesaid scenarios depicts the true facts of the case, I would lay my bets on the Scenario number three.

A few other related questions arise. Nehru was a committed socialist but did he perhaps worry that were he to open up the Indian economy or make it move closer to the capitalist model, the Soviets would not be pleased? Did he think it was better to play safe, as far as the Soviets were concerned? These are valid questions for which there can be no answers, Nehru's thoughts in this regard having died with him.

11. Did The British Know That Bose Was In the Soviet Union? If So, Why Did They Task Their Intelligence Services to Examine the Plane Crash Theory?

The Soviets and the British came to an agreement that they would keep this information (that Bose was in the USSR) under wraps. It would have raised suspicious if the British accepted the air crash theory too easily. So they went through the motions of doing an enquiry to convince an alert Indian audience that they, the British, were genuinely not sure about what had happened to Bose. The results of the enquiry were however pre-determined and the investigators werc instructed that there were orders from the very top that in the end the investigators would have to conclude that there had indeed been an air crash in which Bose had died.

If the British knew that Bose was in the Soviet Union, why did they bother to initiate an enquiry into his disappearance?

The truth of the matter is that the British enquiries were red her rings, meant to convince the general public in India and the world that they, the British, themselves were uncertain about what had happened to Bose.

From the English point of view Bose had proven himself to be a nuisance, far more than say Gandhi or Nehru who had both supported the Allied powers against the Axis powers. Bose was a nuisance but he was a hero to many people in India and a mass leader compared to Nehru. The British far preferred having to deal with the non-violent approach of Gandhi and Nehru. Bose was not inherently against non-violence. From the perspective of the British, Bose was a loose cannon and not reliable in any sense. He was also clever and from the British point of view 'devious' for had he not given them the slip in 1941 and escaped to

Germany? For this reason the British decided that there was no need to declare that Bose was alive, and in the custody of the Soviets. Commencing a trial against him and accusing him of being a war criminal would bring them no advantage; the argument that Bose was a nationalist and a hero only fighting for his country's freedom was not an easy one to counter.

Bose was no prize war criminal in the sense in which Goebbels or Himmler; he was if anything only an Indian patriot. Why not just let him rot inside a Soviet jail for the time being? There was absolutely no rush to set him free. They might have said to Stalin in the British way; 'If you will not hand him over to us, could you just let him cool his military heels in chokey for a while?' Stalin would have happily obliged. That had in any case been his intention all along.

Once Nehru had Taken the Decision….

Once Nehru had taken this fateful decision it subsequently became much more difficult for him to backtrack. The more time passed the more difficult it became. If he got the Soviets to release a statement with respect to his natural death while there, everyone would ask – what took the Soviet's so long, Nehru? Were you the one holding back the disclosures till now? If so, why so? Suspicions would mount. Nehru would be called upon to provide explanations, but no matter what he said, the suspicions both of him and the Soviet Union would only escalate further.

His position as prime minister, the public adulation of *chacha* Nehru, his great dreams of carrying out socialism his way – all this would be threatened. And yet idealistic and lofty minded Nehru perhaps kept thinking to himself that he had withheld the information in public interest. He must have solely missed Gandhi at these moments of confusion; there was no one else in the whole wide world whose opinion on the morality and ethicality of what he was doing he would trust more. But Gandhi was no longer there to guide and give advice.

And so the years passed.

What Papers had Morarji Desai Seen? Why Did Prime Minister Desai Not Follow Up on his Bold Statement in Parliament?

Very many papers related to Bose were destroyed, but there were some communications from the Soviets that were kept well preserved and safe. There were excellent reasons why these papers were not destroyed.

What were these communications and why were they not destroyed? Why could even Nehru and his daughter Indira never contemplate destroying them?

These were letters from the Soviet leadership addressed to Nehru explaining to him that Bose had already died prior to India's independence while it was still a British colony.

These letters clearly exonerated Nehru from any wrong doing. Why were they not destroyed by Nehru and Indira Gandhi? These documents, together with Nehru's response, constituted proof of the prime minister's innocence in respect of charges of criminality that could be potentially levelled against him at a further date. What were these charges?

The first charge that has been levelled against Nehru is that he learnt from the Soviets that Bose was alive and well, and they asked him to let them know what he wished to be done with him. Nehru asked the Soviets to keep Bose incarcerated. This is a serious, criminal charge, which is indefensible, and would permanently cloud Nehru's position in history. This charge has been levelled against him by his enemies and detractors. Nehru may have had his weaknesses, but he would have never done this to his old comrade, regardless of their differences.

The second charge that can potentially be levelled against Nehru is even more serious. It has in fact been levelled against him by Nehru haters such as the BJP Member of Parliament, Subramanian Swamy. Upon learning from the Soviets that Bose was alive and well, instead of asking them to (a) release him or (b) keep him in custody, the prime minister suggested that he be exterminated. This is potentially a murder charge against one of India's great heroes and freedom fighters.

Nehru knew, as his daughter Indira did, that sometime in the future the truth may surface. It was necessary to preserve documents in top secret government records that worked as an alibi for Nehru and were proof of his innocence. Nehru may have been wrong in what he did, and his personal interest may have also played some role, but he was not such a villain. He has his own claim to greatness, of a sort.

When Morarji Desai as the Prime Minister of a non-Congress government came across these papers he was astounded. It was only at the level of the prime minister that he had the clearance to see these top secret papers. The shock of this momentous discovery led him to make his famous statement in Parliament that he had come across new documents that challenged the veracity of the theory of an air crash in Taipei. After making the statement, he reconsidered. He had to weigh the damage to Nehru's reputation, and the consequential damage to the Indian National Congress, Nehru's party, with potential damage to relations with the Soviets and the British. Nehru had a reasonable alibi. Bose was dead in any case. Why endanger India's relations with powerful countries?! On balance, Prime Minister Desai considered that nothing would be gained from disclosing the truth at this late stage.

Do those papers still exist? Undoubtedly, they do! It's a moot question though whether they exist in the government archives or whether they have been shifted to a safe in Sonia Gandhi's house.Certainly, the Gandhi family would have copies of all-important correspondence, if not the original documents.

Chapter - 12

The Real Crime Against Bose

The Pan-Indian Nature of the INA

Could it be said that the Indian National Army had more Southerners in it as compared with the British Indian Army? Not necessarily. It is true that there were more people from Tamil Nadu and other southern states who lived in Singapore and Malaya (later Malaysia) and therefore there would naturally be a greater Southern component to the INA for this reason. It is also however true that many British Indian Prisoners of War who were captured by the Japanese and later enlisted with the INA came from the North. And so it would be truer to say that the INA had a pan Indian nature. In India, as elsewhere in the world, there is a tendency for a family to have more than one boy join the army. In a supreme irony, some of the Indian POW's captured by the Japanese after having joined the INA would have fought against their real brothers who may have been fighting on behalf of the British Indian army in the Burma campaign.

Nehru's Real Crime

Nehru's real crime was to ignore Subhash Bose's great contribution to India's independence. This too was a lesser crime, compared to how he ignored the contributions of the Indian National Army.

Before we criticise Nehru any further we need to look at ourselves. There is nothing wrong in the great national curiosity we possess on what happened to the great man, but it is a tragedy that the issue has become so politicized and a still greater tragedy that we consider that discovery to be *more* important than salvaging the reputation of the INA in our history text books, or paying tribute to them, of having memorials that honour INA leaders and martyrs who died fighting in the cause of Indian independence.

I have little doubt that although Netaji may have been gratified at the attention he has received with regard to his disappearance he would have been mortified to see how he, as a representative of the INA, and the INA itself have been ignored in India's history written by Indians themselves.

Rudrangs hu Mukerjee, author of a book comparing the two personalities, Bose and Nehru writes: 'The most exciting period of Subhash's life was in sharp contrast with the most dull periods in Jawaharlal's. The principal reason for this was the fact that from 9 April 1992 to 15 June, 1945, he was in prison – his longest term, 1040 days.'[270] Nehru was devoted to Gandhi but perhaps he also saw that unlike Bose, who could go his own way, he did not have a real political future without the Mahatma's blessings. Nehru's closeness to Gandhi (despite their differences), Mukerjee suggests was perhaps 'an admission of his own shortcomings as a mass leader.'[271]

It is a sad and terrible truth that in revolutions around the world, thousands of people take part in the effort but when the great day finally arrives, oftentimes an over-ambitious section within the revolutionaries decides to take all the credit, and seize the reins of power. Those revolutionaries, who gave their all for the cause, but have been left out in the cold, by those with whom they once walked shoulder to shoulder, become sad, embittered individuals. In many cases they had no lust for power; all that they wanted was a thank you, a medal, even if it were made of tin, as an acknowledgement of their sacrifices.

In the case of India's struggle for freedom, truth be told, the situation is hardly different. Nehru became prime minister and the Congress Party seized power. There was nothing wrong with that in itself, but they ignored those others who weren't part of the 'team' so to speak, but were nonetheless part of the broader effort with incredible sacrifices made for the cause.

Yes, it is tragic that Nehru did not hoist even a portrait of Netaji in the Central Halls of the Indian Parliament, but the tragedy lies only in part in ignoring the man himself. Why focus on Netaji alone? None of the other heroes of the Indian National Army have their portrait there either. Even a portrait of the Rani of Jhansi regiment is missing! The real tragedy is that Nehru, the Congress and successive governments have not only ignored Bose, they have deliberately ignored the sacrifices made by the men and women of the Indian National Army that Bose commanded.

There are many who write with a great deal of truth that it was because of Netaji's and the INA's efforts that the British left. There are reports that suggest that Clement Attlee the British Prime Minister at the time of Indian independence attributed the departure of the British to Bose and the Indian National Army.[272] Although the INA had been defeated in the world war, a new spirit and consciousness had arisen across the country, most visible during the celebrated INA trials at the Red Fort. When Attlee was asked how much Gandhi had influenced the British decision, his response had been brief and sarcastic. 'Minimal,' he said.

Be that as it may should we, as a nation, be reduced to squabbling about whose contribution was the greater, the Congress's or the Indian National Army's. They both worked for the cause and Subhash Bose never lost sight of the fact that he believed that his cause – freedom from British rule – was also being fought by the likes of Gandhi and Nehru. Regiments were named after Gandhi and Nehru in the INA. Bose gave them full credit, but alas, they did not give *him* his due.

It is sign of shameful pettiness to not share credit with others who have worked towards the same cause. Forget a great national struggle, even a film director must thank his entire team of actors and assistants, a singer must acknowledge the music director and lyricist. Something truly substantial is rarely if ever accomplished alone, and even in those cases where it is, credit must be given by such an achiever to those before him who inspired him. How terrible and shameful therefore that Nehru and the Congress hogged all the limelight.

Did they provide any justification for doing so? Some did, rather disingenuously. The main argument advanced is: Nehru was a true democrat, Netaji a man with dictatorial tendencies. What proof do they offer for this bald assertion? They pull out some of Subhash Bose's statements out of context to make this argument. As further proof they speak of his alliance with the great dictators of the time, Hitler and Mussolini. Two plus two makes twenty two in their arithmetic, and since Bose was allied with dictators he must therefore himself perforce be a dictator. This is a patently false and despicable allegation to make against Bose! Surviving women from the INA's Rani of Jhansi Regiment recall how upon the INA's defeat he insisted that he would be the last man out and sent them all to safety ahead of himself.[273] This is how democrats behave, even in the time of war.

Poor Netaji had no choice in this matter. The enemy of my enemy is my enemy; that was his motif. Even had they not been fascists but cannibals he would not have hesitated to team up with them! It is natural for the English and the Americans to accuse Bose of teaming up with fascists, but it is a shame that our own Indian historians followed the same colonised historical mindset. Did not the English and the Americans team up with the Soviets, an ideological foe, in order to defeat Hitler and forces aligned themselves with him? As far as the Americans were concerned, it could even be argued that history would show how they despised the communist system even more than ordinary dictatorships.

People who live in glass houses ought not to throw stones. Did the Mahatma himself not display the tendencies of the dictator when he went on his numerous fasts and practically blackmailed the nation into doing his bidding? Did Nehru not display great lust for power when he refused to play second fiddle to Patel and to share the limelight with others? Did Nehru ever stop the

Congress machine from building him up as a larger than life figure? Did this image building exercise not simultaneously heartlessly ignore others who made great contributions to the cause of Indian freedom? And even if, even if, only for the sake of argument, we do acknowledge for a second that yes, possibly Netaji too had an element of the dictator within him, is it fair to contemptuously dismiss the contributions of allthose thousands of other brave sons and daughters of Mother India who, under Bose's leadership, gave their all and laid down their lives for the country. Is the suggestion that a dictatorial streak may have lain somewhere within the heart of their leader sufficient to discredit and rubbish *their* contributions?!

The image of the Unknown Soldier at India Gate may represent those who were aligned with the Congress on three days of the weeks, but the other four days of the week, that face is that of the soldier who fought in the trenches and jungles of Burma on behalf of the Indian National Army.

The famous singer Lata Mangeshkar once sang a song in front of Prime Minister Nehru, the penultimate lines of which runs something like this:

Aye, Merayvatan key logon,

Jaraaankhmeybhar lo pani,

Jo shaheed hua hain unki

Jara yaad karo kurbani

Or, in my somewhat defective translation:

Oh, the People of my Country

Will ye not fill your eyes with tears?

For those who were martyred in the cause of our freedom

And pause momentarily to remember that sacrifice.

Nehru wept. Were his tears only for the soon-to-be-corrupted foot soldiers of the Congress, and for those who fought the wars of the British occupiers? Was there any sorrow in his heart for the proud soldiers of the Indian National Army? Did even a single tear fall on account of the contributions of martyred Bose and his INA comrades?

Acknowledge Mahatma Gandhi as the father of the nation by all means! He deserves that position but remember too the man who coined that epithet for him: Bose. Give Nehru credit too for his secular mindedness, his nurturing of democratic institutions, and his thoughtfulness in many matters! Give others in the Congress due credit. But, but… please…spare some space on the stage where so-called warriors of Indian independence have gathered and let some of the spot light fall also on the noble and valiant men and women of the Indian National Army who gave their lives for the cause of Indian independence!

There is credit enough to go around and be shared. We are not so poor in spirit or heart as a nation.

History taught in our schools and universities focuses almost entirely on how Gandhi led the freedom movement and the Indian National Congress in a non-violent struggle against the British. In this he was ably supported by Sardar Vallabh Bhai Patel, and Pandit Jawaharlal Nehru, India's first prime minister.

Perhaps the history text would be fairer and more accurate if it spoke in grand terms of the non-violent struggle led by Gandhi, the burning of foreign clothing, the encouragement of the use of *khadi*, the launch of a non-cooperation movement, and so on. And then our history would also speak of how an equivalent struggle was also waged outside the country where Subhash Chandra Bose, previously a President of the Indian National Congress founded the Indian National Army which aligned itself with the Japanese and the Germans under Bose's idea and banner that 'the enemy of my enemy is my friend.'

It is unseemly to find people squabbling amongst themselves about whose contribution to the great cause of Indian independence was the greater. Let me give the reader an illustration of what I mean to say!

A few white rats get into a house full of thousands of brown mice. The white rats being bigger and more powerful take charge of the house and command the timid mice to do their bidding, which they do for many years. Over time however some mice rebel and refuse to do the rats bidding anymore. More and more of the brown mice are pulled to the movement known as 'non-cooperation'. Meanwhile a few hundred mice escape from the house, team up with other mice in the neighbourhood and start to give the house a good shake from the outside. Inside the house, the white rats confer hurriedly. The provisions inside the house have mostly already been looted and little remains. They are increasingly disturbed by the mice inside the house who are not offering any cooperation and the mice outside who are shaking the house. They decide to leave. Only the white rats themselves know which mice troubled them more. Once they leave the brown mice inside the house take charge, take full credit for getting rid of the white rats, and assume control of the house. The brown mice who worked so hard from the outside are completely ignored.

* * *

Declassification of Files May Spoil India's Relations with Foreign Powers

Initially, just like previous governments the Modi government too took the stance that declassification of the Netaji files could possibly spoil our relations with other countries. The grounds given by the Minister of State for Home Affairs, Mr Haribhai Chaudhury were that the files were of a 'sensitive nature' and could pose a problem 'for India's relations with foreign countries'[274].

The precisely worded statement reads as follows:

'The Ministry of External Affairs has informed (me) that the information contained in these files is of a sensitive nature and bringing this information in the public domain at this juncture is not desirable from the point of view of India's relations with other countries.'[275]

How is one to interpret such a statement by the Indian government? What does this really mean? Why will it spoil relations? There can be only one meaning of this. Normally when relations are spoiled between Country A and Country B it is because Country A comes to know that Country B has said or done something against it or vice versa. It is beyond the bounds of probability that Bose, or his compatriots had done something to these countries that could potentially poison mutual relations. What could the servant/slave nation have done that could endanger mutual relations?!

It is therefore practically a certainty that some other country (the most likely candidates are Britain and Russia) *did* something to Bose, a national hero, the revelation of which would anger the Indian people to such an extent that it could affect mutual relations. It is also clear that the planning by the British to assassinate Nehru will not count for much in the general scheme of things. This is information that has already entered the public domain – that the British had hatched a plot to assassinate Subhash Chandra Bose – and did not create any ripples. So, some country, Country A,either alone or in collusion with country Country B 'did' something to Bose…..

Should the history of our independence be allowed to remain incomplete or falsified because we don't want to risk affecting our relationship with certain unknown countries? Are we not a free nation even now? Would the British or Russian public ever tolerate suppression of information on the ground that it might affect relations with India? We have not just become independent. If we have not allowed massacres such as the Jallianwallah Bagh massacre to affect friendly ties with Britain, why should we worry at this stage, seventy long years since independence?

Who Were Braver – The British Indian Army or The INA Soldiers?

We are now nearing the end of this book and it is time to ask some difficult, even painful questions.

The soldiers of the Indian National Army (INA) who were brought back to India to face trial were ultimately given a reprieve.

This was not done out of the goodness of the Englishman's heart, but rather because there was a strong groundswell of Indian public opinion in their favour which could not be ignored. Had it been only the Indian civilian population who were outraged at the trial the British might have not cared, but there was clear support for the INA even among the ranks of the British Indian army. The British may have consulted with the Congress Party but the party too threw up their hands. The issue was such that the Congress could not go against the tide of public opinion, otherwise it would itself lose favour. The British understood that they could have a rebellion in the Indian army on their hands if they did not proceed with care and caution.

After sacrificing thousands of lives for the British in their war, why was it that on the INA issue, the British Indian army was suddenly no longer loyal to the British or could not be trusted to remain loyal?

Sections of the British Indian army started to question themselves and their own motivations when they came into conflict with their own Indian brothers serving in the INA in the North East and in Burma. Their conscience was troubled and their intellect finally awakened. How could they possibly fight with and kill their own Indian brothers, *who were fighting for India's independence.* Whether the Japanese could be trusted was a separate, intellectual question really. The Indians fighting for the INA were fighting for India's independence. Who was the British Indian army fighting for? It was for the British. They could not find it within themselves to refute the greater logic to INA actions. India had not even been promised freedom by the British. Why were they fighting? Were there not mercenaries compared with the INA? Such were the troubling questions that passed through each British Indian army soldier's mind, and there was no satisfactory answer. They were also fighting against people whom they knew and had fought alongside. Those very men from the British Indian Army now worked in service of the INA.

When Indians fought for the British in conflicts far away in Europe and in Africa, they probably did not even ask themselves such troubling questions. Why am I fighting? Why, in God's name, am I risking my life fighting for a race that rules over my own people, who humiliate and disrespect them day in and day out? They were somehow able to ignore such questions from raising their head, because they were fighting against people they didn't know. The enemy, be it African or European was really an abstraction.

Face to face with their brothers (and even sisters!!) in the INA they could not ignore these questions. The question of fighting against the Ranis from Bose's Jhansi of Rani Regiment would not have been merely troubling; it would have been heart-breaking for any uniformed Indian with honour, chivalry and self-respect! Doubts spread within the ranks of the British army not only engaged in the north east and in Burma but across the country even as they won the war and the INA was forced to retreat.

Families in India continue to celebrate the courage displayed by their ancestors in wars fought on behalf of the British. Is it worth celebrating really? Is it not the courage of a mercenary that is being celebrated?

Courage is always worth celebrating, it may be said, with truth, even if it the courage of a mercenary. Let us also not forget that the idea of Indian nationalism had still to be properly formed. The Indians who fought for the British fought as they would have for any other king.

That is true, but on the other hand surely the courage of a person who fights for a noble cause is on a higher footing. The courage of a person who fought for a foreign English queen must be judged at a lower level than the courage of a man or a woman who fought for the freedom of India? Even the British admired the courage of the famed Rani of Jhansi, more than they admired the courage of their own men, be they English or Indian.[276]

There will be some who will argue, with a degree of justice that there were mercenaries with in the INA too. It is true that there were many British Indian Prisoners of War who had been captured by the Japanese. Netaji met these men and convinced them that they had all along been fighting with the wrong people for a cause that was not their own; many saw the logic in his arguments and agreed to enlist in the INA to fight against the British. They were then no longer treated as Prisoners of War and became a fighting asset for Bose and the Japanese. Now it could be said that some of these men were no better than mercenaries, and their real motive was not to remain Prisoners of War anymore, but to have their freedom as a soldier. No one can delve into the secret corners of the hearts of these men and know the purity of their reformed understanding: was it just the better life and freedom of a soldier that they coveted, or were they now really seeing the foolishness of their earlier ways? They were in any event willing to risk their lives. Even Shah Nawaz, the chairman of the first committee that enquired into the alleged air crash in which Bose was supposed to have died was one such individual, who had been 'converted' to the INA cause. He had originally fought with the British Indian Army, had been captured by the Japanese, made a Prisoner of War, and then after listening to Subhash Bose's inspiring talk he returned to the theatre of war but this time to fight *against* the British. There were many such converts, and the purity of their actions may have been uncertain or questionable in some cases.

On the other hand there were also thousands of men and women who fought for the INA, who had no prior military experience. These were men and women who had not fought in any army. No woman soldier in the INA's Rani of Jhansi regiment (named after the legendary heroine of the 1857 rebellion) had ever fought a war before but they had been drawn to the cause by Bose's stirring words. This was heroism at another level altogether, rarely surpassed anywhere in the world. There are numerous moving testimonies of parents in Singapore and Malaysia giving permission to their daughters, upon Netaji's request to fight in the great Indian cause of freedom. We need to honour not only the ladies who died fighting, the women who survived, but also their beloved parents and families who consented to have their daughters risk their lives.

Netaji never had a portrait in the Indian Parliament for many years. A great affront to one of India's great sons, but it could have been ignored if it had been the only one, and other heroes from the INA had been honoured. No one was honoured. Yet more shamefully, not a single Rani has been honoured. They deserve not only a standalone group photograph placed in a corner but they deserve an entire wall – and even that would not suffice to properly honour them!

Notes

1. Hugh Toye, 'Subhash Chandra Bose: The Springing Tiger,' Jaico Publishing House, 1991
2. John Le Carre, 'The Spy Who Came in From the Cold' Penguin Modern Classics, UK; 2010
3. India Today issue dated 20 April, 2015 titled 'Snooping on Netaji…' page 24
4. Lead Story in India Today issue dated 20 April, 2015 titled 'Snooping on Netaji: How Nehru's government spied on Subhash Chandra Bose's kin for nearly twenty years.'
5. Leonard Gordan, 'Brothers Against the Raj: A biography of Indian nationalists Sarat and Subhash Chandra Bose,' Columbia University Press, 1999
6. Ibid
7. G D Khosla, 'Indira Gandhi' Thompson Press India, Publications Division, 1974
8. Rajmohan Gandhi, 'Patel: A Life,' Navjivan Trust; 2011
9. Philip Oldenburg, 'The Thirteenth Election of India's Lok Sabha,' The Asia Society; September, 1999
10. Leonard Gordan, 'Brothers Against the Raj: A biography of Indian nationalists Sarat and Subhash Chandra Bose,' Columbia University Press, 1999
11. Ernest Renan, 'What is a Nation?', text of a conference delivered at the Sorbonne on March 11th 1882, in Ernest Renan, 'Qu est-cequ'une nation,' Paris, Presses-Pocket, 1992 (translated by Ethan Rundell)
12. Sagari Chhabra, 'In Search of Freedom,' Harper Collins India, 2015
13. Note: Sagari Chhabra's 'In Search of Freedom,' (Harper Collins India, 2015) contains testimonies of many INA men and women who fought for Indian independence. Most of these freedom fighters do not draw a pension, some suffer penury, many in Myanmar are stateless persons and do not even have a passport.
14. Javier Moro, 'The Red Sari: A Dramatized Biography of Sonia Gandhi,' Roli Books; 2015
15. Sunil Khilnani, 'The Idea of India,' Penguin India, 1997 at page 27

16. Tapati Dasgupta, 'Social Thought of Rabindranath Tagore: A Historical Analysis,' Abhinav Publications, 1993 at page 188
17. RudrangshuMukerjee, 'Nehru and Bose: Parallel Lives' Penguin Viking, 2014 at page 198
18. Rudrangshu Mukerjee, 'Nehru and Bose: Parallel Lives' Penguin Viking, 2014 at page 198
19. Ibid: at 199
20. Letter to Emilie, 14 May, 1939, in *Netaji: Collected Works,* volume 7 page 212
21. Letter to Emilie, 16 June, 1939, in ibid, page 213
22. Sandip Rai, 'Nehru got Netaji executed: Swamy,' *The Times of India,* 23 January, 2015
23. Marshall J Getz, 'Subhash Chandra Bose: A Biography,' MacFarland and Company, Jefferson, NC, 2002
24. B R Ambedkar, 'What Congress and Gandhi have done to the Untouchables,' page 1 Source: www.ambedkar.org
25. Srikant Prasoon (ed.), 'My Letters – MK Gandhi,' Cedar Books, 2013 at page 71
26. Ibid; 377
27. Ibid; at page 371
28. As quoted in Sandeep Unnithan, 'When Nehru Spied on Netaji,' India Today, April 20, 2015 at page 28
29. See YouTube link of interview of BR Ambedkar on BBC at: *www.**youtube**.com/watch?v=ZJs-BJoSzbo*
30. Prof. Srikant Prasoon, ed, 'My Letters – MK Gandhi,' Cedar Books, 2011; at page 275
31. Alex Von Tunzelmann, ' Indian Summer: The Secret History of the End of an Empire,' Simon and Schuster, 2008
32. Mridula Mukherjee, 'A Misguided Patriot' *India Today*, 20 April, 2015 at page 32
33. Arun Shourie, 'Eminent Historians: Their Technology, their Line, their Fraud,' Harper Collins Publishers India Ltd, 2014
34. Dominique Lapierre and Larry Collins, 'Freedom at Midnight,' Vikas Publishing House, 2011
35. Suresh Chandra Basu, 'The Dissentient Report,' page 26
36. Note: It is true of course that Gandhi wore the military uniform in his younger days and saw action in the Boer War and the Zulu uprising
37. Extract from Hugh Toye's 'Subhash Chandra Bose, The Springing Tiger, page 74
38. Vikas Pathak, 'Nehru arranged financial support for Netaji's wife and daughter,' *The Hindu,* 24 January, 2016
39. Ramachandra Guha, 'Soldiers of the Nation: Towards a Bose-Gandhi reconciliation,' *The Telegraph,* 21 January, 2017
40. Sagari Chhabra, 'In Search of Freedom: Travels through South East Asia,' Harper Collins, 2015

41. Ramachandra Guha, 'Soldiers of the Nation: Towards a Bose-Gandhi reconciliation,' *The Telegraph,* 21 January, 2017
42. Sandeep Unnithan, 'When Nehru Spied on Netaji,' India Today, April 20, 2015 at page 29
43. Note: Sisir Kumar Basu was close to Netaji. The India Today issue states that he drove Netaji from Kolkotta to Gomoh from where he boarded a train to Peshawar during his 1941 escape. Emilie's letter suggests closeness; it may have been the reason why the government thought he would be a likely person to persuade the family to bring back the ashes.
44. Sandeep Unnithan, 'When Nehru Spied on Netaji,' India Today, April 20, 2015 at page 22
45. Ibid
46. Ibid
47. Ibid: at page 24
48. Ibid
49. Ibid: at page 28
50. Ibid
51. Ibid; at page 29
52. Ibid; at page 30
53. Ibid; at page 30- 31
54. Ibid; at page 31
55. Nigel West, 'The Guy Liddel Diaries,' Routledge, 2009
56. Pradip Basu, 'Towards Naxalbari: An Account of Inner-Party Ideological Struggle,' Progressive Publishers, 2000
57. Sandeep Unnithan, 'When Nehru Spied on Netaji,' India Today, April 20, 2015 at page 28
58. B N Mullick, 'My Years with Nehru,' Allied Publishers, 1971
59. Source: Wikipedia – Death of Subhash Chandra Bose
60. Sandeep Unnithan, 'When Nehru Spied on Netaji,' India Today, April 20, 2015 at page 30
61. Ibid; at page 29
62. Ibid; at page 30
63. Letter to his brother from Inseon Jail cited in Hugh Toye, 'Subhash Chandra Bose: The Springing Tiger,' Jaico Publishing House, 1991; page 48
64. Hugh Toye, 'Subhash Chandra Bose: The Springing Tiger,' Jaico Publishing House, 1991; page 18
65. Ibid; page 5
66. Justice Mukherjee Commission Report at page 1
67. Suresh Chandra Basu, 'The Dissentient Report,' page 26
68. Justice Mukherjee Commission Report at page 1
69. Ragini Bhuyan, 'Legacy wrapped in a mystery,' The Hindu Business Line, 17 July, 2015

70. Suresh Chandra Basu, 'The Dissentient Report,' page 26
71. Ibid
72. Justice Mukherjee Commission Report at page 1
73. Suresh Chandra Basu, 'The Dissentient Report,' page 57
74. Ibid
75. Anuj Dhar, 'No Secrets, Vitasta Publishing Private Limited, Delhi; 2013 at page
76. 'BJP Leader L K Advani sole leader to pay homage to Netaji Subhash Chandra Bose at Parliament House,' 23 January, 2014, *The Economic Times*
77. Anuj Dhar, No Secrets, at page 143
78. Suresh Chandra Basu, 'The Dissentient Report,' page 3
79. Ibid; at page 4
80. India Today issue dated 20 April, 2015 titled 'Snooping on Netaji' at page 25
81. Suresh Chandra Basu, 'The Dissentient Report,' page 70
82. Ibid
83. Suresh Chandra Basu, 'The Dissentient Report,' page 80
84. Ibid; page 82
85. Ibid
86. Ibid
87. Ibid: page 3
88. Ibid; page 79
89. Ibid; page 42
90. Ibid; page 44
91. Ibid
92. Ibid; page 43
93. Ibid; page 92
94. Ibid
95. Ibid
96. Ibid; page 47
97. Ibid; page 50
98. Ibid; page 55
99. Ibid
100. Ibid
101. Ibid
102. Ibid; page 59
103. Ibid
104. Ibid; page 60 – Note: The nurse's testimony was not given to the Commission. It was referred to in the testimony of Mr Harin Shah, a journalist.
105. Ibid.
106. Ibid; page 59-60
107. Ibid; page 54
108. Ibid; page 9

109. Ibid
110. 'Hamlet' is said to have been written in 1599/1600
111. Ibid; page 10
112. Suresh Chandra Basu, 'The Dissentient Report,' page 11
113. Manimughda Sharma, 'Meet Sergeant Major Mohandas Karamchand Gandhi,' *The Times of India,* 2 October, 2014
114. 'The Most Punctual Man in India,' Lapham's Quarterly, 2 December, 2014
115. Suresh Chandra Basu, 'The Dissentient Report,' page 22
116. Sagari Chhabra, 'In Search of Freedom: Travels through South East Asia,' Harper Collins, 2015
117. Suresh Chandra Basu, 'The Dissentient Report; page 70
118. Ibid; page 71
119. Letter no SLO/CS/1 dated 1.3.46
120. Ibid; page 68
121. Ibid
122. Letter to his brother from Inseon Jail cited in Hugh Toye, 'Subhash Chandra Bose: The Springing Tiger,' Jaico Publishing House, 1991; page 48
123. Ramachandra Guha, 'Patriots and Partisans,' Penguin India; 2013
124. Notification dated July 11, 1970
125. Hugh Toye, 'Subhash Chandra Bose: The Springing Tiger,' Jaico Publishing House, 1991; page 48
126. Leonard Gordan, 'Brothers Against the Raj: A biography of Indian nationalists Sarat and Subhash Chandra Bose,' Columbia University Press, 1999
127. Hugh Toye, 'Subhash Chandra Bose: The Springing Tiger,' Jaico Publishing House, 1991; page 4
128. G D Khosla, 'Indira Gandhi' Thompson Press India, Publications Division, 1974
129. Attributed to Judge Henry Cecil
130. Report of Justice Mukherjee Commission;
131. High Court order dated 30 April, 1998
132. Resolution of the West Bengal Assembly dated 24 December, 1998
133. Report of Justice Mukherjee Commission; at page
134. Smita Gupta, 'BJP strikes a note of caution,' The Hindu, 20 September, 2015
135. Report of Justice Mukherjee Commission;
136. Section 3 provides as follows:

    3. *Appointment of Commission. (1) The appropriate Government may, if it is of opinion that it is necessary so to do, and shall, if a resolution in this behalf is passed by each House of Parliament or, as the case may be, the Legislature of the State by notification in the official Gazette, appoint a Commission of Inquiry for the purpose of making an inquiry into any definite matter of public importance and performing such functions and within such time as may be specified in the notification, and the Commission so appointed shall make the inquiry and perform the functions accordingly.*

Section 2 of the Act defines the appropriate government as follows:

2. *Definitions. In this Act, unless the context otherwise requires,-*

(a) "Appropriate Government" means-

(i) the Central Government, in relation to a Commission appointed by it to make an inquiry into any matter relatable to any of the entries enumerated in List I or List II or List III in the Seventh Schedule to the Constitution ; and

(ii) the State Government, in relation to a Commission appointed by it to make an inquiry into any matter relatable to any of the entries enumerated in List II or List III in the Seventh Schedule to the Constitution

(Note: the Act gives the Central Government the power even with respect to List 2…)

137. Notification dated May 14, 1999.

138. I have only slightly paraphrased the questions in the interests of greater readability.

139. 3 December, 1999

140. Section 8 B of the Commission of Inquiry Act, 1952 provide as follows:

8.B. Persons likely to be prejudicially affected to be heard.

If, at any stage of the inquiry, the Commission,—

(a) considers it necessary to inquire into the conduct of any person ; or

(b) is of opinion that the reputation of any person is likely to be prejudicially affected by the inquiry, the Commission shall give to that person a reasonable opportunity of being heard in the inquiry and to produce evidence in his defence:

Provided that nothing in this section shall apply where the credit of a witness is being impeached.

141. Statistical report on Election in the State of West Bengal, 2001, Election Commission of India.

142. File no. 12(226)/56-PM

143. Order dated 23rd March 2000

144. Letter dated May 2, 2000

145. Mukherjee Commission Report: Director of PMO's letter dated July 4, 2000 which referred to file No.12(226)/56-PM which contained agenda paper/cabinet decision regarding ''investigation into the circumstances leading to the death of Shri Subhas Chandra Bose"

146. Dan Roberts, 'Clapper under pressure despite apology for erroneous statements to Congress,' *The Guardian,* 1 July, 2013

147. Ibid

148. Mukherjee Commission Report: Letter dated 21 September, 2000 issued by the Commission to the Prime Minister's Secretariat

149. Letter dated 3 January, 1974.

150. Mukherjee Commission Report.

151. Mukherjee Commission Report: Statement issued by Morarji Desai on August 28, 1978

152. Statement of Prime Minister Morarji Desai is recorded at pages 455 and 456 of the Parliamentary proceedings dated August 28, 1978.

153. The powers of the Commission are spelled out in Section 4 of the Act as follows:

    4. Powers of Commission.

    The Commission shall have the powers of a civil court, while trying a suit under the Code of Civil Procedure, 1908, in respect of the following matters, namely:

    (a) summoning and enforcing the attendance of any person from any part of India] and examining him on oath;

    (b) requiring the discovery and production of any document

    (c) receiving evidence on affidavits;

    (d) requisitioning any public record or copy thereof from any court of office;

    (e) issuing commissions for the examination of witnesses or documents ;

    (f) any other matter which may be prescribed.

154. Section 5 (4) provides as follows:

    5(4) The Commission shall be deemed to be a civil court and when any offence as is described in section 175, section 178, section 179, section 180 or section 228 of the Indian Penal Code (45 of 1860)is committed in the view or presence of the Commission, the Commission may, after recording the facts constituting the offence and the statement of the accused as provided for in the Code of Criminal Procedure, 1898, (5 of 1898) forward the case to a magistrate having jurisdiction to try the same and the magistrate to whom any such case is forwarded shall proceed to hear the complaint against the accused as if the case had been forwarded to him under section 482 of the Code of the Criminal Procedure, 1898.

    (5) Any proceeding before the Commission shall be deemed to be a judicial proceeding within the meaning of sections 193 and 228 of the Indian Penal Code.(45 of 1860).

155. Ibid.

156. Section 175 IPC - Omission to produce document to public servant by person legally bound to produce it.

    Whoever, being legally bound to produce or deliver up any document of any public servant, as such, intentionally omits so to produce or deliver up the same, shall be punished with simple imprisonment for a term which may extend to one month, or with fine which may extend to five hundred rupees, or with both, or, if the document is to be produced or delivered up to a Court of Justice, with simple imprisonment for a term which may extend to six months, or with fine which may extend to one thousand rupees, or with both.

157. Section 193 IPC –193. Punishment for false evidence

    Whoever intentionally gives false evidence in any stage of a judicial proceeding, or fabricates false evidence for the purpose of being used in any stage of a judicial proceeding, shall be punished with imprisonment of either description for a term which may extend to seven years, and shall also be liable to fine, and whoever intentionally gives or fabricates false evidence in any other case, shall be punished with imprisonment of either description for a term which may extend to three years, and shall also be liable to fine.

158. Note: Especially notable among the RTI activists is journalist and campaigner Anuj Dhar, who amassed a great deal of information and authored two books on Netaji and his disappearance.
159. Mukherjee Commission Report
160. Mukherjee Commission Report: Letter dated December 18, 2001 from the MEA
161. Anuj Dhar, 'No Secrets,'
162. Mukherjee Commission Report
163. Mukherjee Commission Report
164. Louis Fischer, 'Life of Mahatma Gandhi,' Harper Collins Publishers; 2004
165. Mukherjee Commission Report
166. Quoted in Hugh Toye, 'Subhash Chandra Bose: The Springing Tiger,' Jaico Publishing House, 1991; page 189.
167. Ibid: a copy of the memorandum is annexed to the report and marked Annexure-C/2.
168. Section 3(4) of the Public Records Act passed by the British Parliament reads as follows:

    (1) It shall be the duty of every person responsible for public records of any description which are not in the Public Record Office or a place of deposit appointed by the Lord Chancellor under this Act to make arrangements for the selection of those records which ought to be permanently preserved and for their safe-keeping.

    (2) Every person shall perform his duties under this section under the guidance of the Keeper of Public Records and the said Keeper shall be responsible for co-ordinating and supervising all action taken under this section.

    (3) All public records created before the year sixteen hundred and sixty shall be included among those selected for permanent preservation.

    (4) Public records selected for permanent preservation under this section shall be transferred not later than thirty years after their creation either to the Public Record Office ***or to such other place of deposit*** *appointed by the Lord Chancellor under this Act as the Lord Chancellor may direct:*

    Provided that any records may be retained after the said period if, in the opinion of the person who is responsible for them, they are required for administrative purposes or ought to be retained for any other special reason and, where that person is not the Lord Chancellor, the Lord Chancellor has been informed of the facts and given his approval

169. Note: Lord Archer, since deceased, was a Labour MP and a peer who fought for human rights.
170. Mukherjee Commission Report
171. Mukherjee Commission Report: Letter dated November 13, 2002 was received from the Minister, a copy of which is annexed to the report and marked Annexure-A/6.
172. Mukherjee Commission Report: Letter from the Joint Secretary dated July 15, 2003

173. Mukherjee Commission Report: British Foreign and Commonwealth Office (FCO) communication dated May 22, 2003
174. Mukherjee Commission Report: Letter from the American Embassy dated May 2, 2001
175. The Ministry's instructions were issued in May 2001
176. Mukherjee Commission Report: Letter from the American Embassy dated June 23, 2003
177. Mukherjee Commission Report: Letters from the Commission dated June 28, 2004
178. Mukherjee Commission Report: Letters from the Commission dated July 6, 2004 and September 2, 2004
179. Mukherjee Commission Report: Annexure C 2
180. Mukherjee Commission Report, in Part 4.10.14
181. Mukherjee Commission Report: Letters from the Commission dated July 6, 2004 and September 2, 2004
182. Navtan Kumar, 'Pressure was put on Netaji's kin to accept crash theory,' Sunday Guardian, 19 April, 2015
183. Ibid
184. Kunal Anand, 'Five Reasons why the Nehru snoop on Netaji is Incredibly Strange,' 10 April 2015, *India Times*. The web link is: http://www.indiatimes.com/news/india/5-reasons-why-the-nehrusnoop-on-netaji-is-incredibly-strange-231768.html
185. Navtan Kumar, 'Pressure was put on Netaji's kin to accept crash theory,' Sunday Guardian, 19 April, 2015
186. Benazir Bhutto, 'Daughter of the East: An Autobiography,' Simon and Schuster, 2008
187. Onishi Norimitsu, 'Decades After War Trials Japan still honours a Dissenting Judge,' The New York Times, 31 August 2007
188. Ibid
189. Anuj Dhar, 'No Secrets,'
190. Suresh Chandra Basu, 'The Dissentient Report,' page 12-13
191. Ibid; page 13
192. Ibid; page 13
193. Sagari Chhabra, 'In Search of Freedom: Travels through South East Asia,' Harper Collins, 2015
194. Suresh Chandra Basu, 'The Dissentient Report,' page 13
195. L C Green, 'The Indian National Army Trials,' Modern Law Review 11 (4): 47–69.
196. Source: History of DNA profiling; University of Leicester
197. Amy Chavez, 'What is Respect for the Aged Day,' Planet Tokyo, 2 September, 2008.
198. Note: Copies of the correspondence referred to above are annexed herewith and marked Annexure B/2 (collectively) of the Mukherjee Commission Report.

199. Source: The Mukherjee Commission's Report. See the Commission's letters dated December 17, 2002 and December 26, 2002 (copies annexed and marked Annexure B/3 collectively).
200. The said letter is marked Annexure B/4 to the Mukherjee Commission Report
201. Schwark T, Heinrich A, 'Reliable Genetic Identification of burnt human remains,'Forensic Science International, 2011, November 5 (5) at pages 393-9
202. Letter from the Director CCMB dated December 10, 2002
203. Copies of the correspondence with the foreign experts as referred to in this paragraph are annexed to the Mukherjee Commission Report and marked Annexure B/5 (collectively).
204. Annexure B/6 to the Mukherjee Commission Report
205. Copies of the letter dated April 10, 2003, (bereft of the relevant enclosures of the letter as already annexed to this report) and the reply received from MHA are annexed to the Mukherjee Commission Report and marked Annexures B/9 & B/10 respectively.
206. Mukherjee Commission Report: Copies of the MEA's letter dated May 31, 2004 and the Commission's letter dated June 17, 2004 are annexed to the report and marked Annexures-B/11 and B/12.
207. Mukherjee Commission Report: Copies of the correspondence referred to above are annexed to the report and marked Annexure B/13 (collectively).
208. Mukherjee Commission Report: Copies of the CCMB's letter dated November 3, 2004 and the Commission's letter dated November 9, 2004 referred to above are annexed to the report and marked Annexure B/14 [collectively]).
209. Mukherjee Commission Report: Copy of MEA's letter dated April 25, 2005 together with enclosures thereof and copies of the Commission's letter dated May 20, 2005 and its reminder dated July 4, 2005 are annexed to the report and marked Annexure B/15 [collectively]).
210. Suresh Chandra Basu, 'The Dissentient Report,' page 63.
211. Ibid; at page 62
212. Ibid; last para at page 62
213. Ibid; at page 63
214. Ibid; at page 63
215. No G-12(3)/98-NGO
216. Navtan Kumar, 'Pressure was put on Netaji's kin to accept crash theory,' *Sunday Guardian*, 19 April, 2015
217. Ibid
218. 'Netaji's daughter wants DNA test of ashes kept in Renkoji Temple, First Post, 26 January, 2016
219. Advances in DNA Profiling, OMICS Group, 2013
220. Ibid
221. Abhinandan Mishra, 'Secretive Babus not ready to shed light on Netaji disappearance,' The Sunday Guardian, 19 April, 2015
222. Ibid: a copy of the memorandum is annexed to the report and marked as Annexure-C/1.

223. Ibid: Not a Court within the meaning of section 3 of the Indian Evidence Act
224. Mukherjee Commission Report
225. Mukherjee Commission Report
226. No crash killing Netaji took place', *Hindustan Times*, 5 February 2005
227. Ibid
228. Ibid
229. Ibid
230. Ibid
231. Ibid
232. Mukherjee Commission Report Annexure D/1
233. Quoted in Hugh Toye, 'Subhash Chandra Bose: The Springing Tiger,' Jaico Publishing House, 1991, at page 25
234. Ibid
235. Ibid
236. Ibid; para 4.5
237. Ibid; CW 33, 63 and 64
238. Ibid; para 4.15.1
239. Ibid; CW 119
240. Ibid; CW 121
241. Ibid; CW 120
242. Ibid; para 4.15.9
243. Rudrangshu Mukerjee, 'Nehru and Bose: Parallel Lives' Penguin Viking, 2014
244. PLeonard Gordan, 'Brothers Against the Raj,' Columbia University Press, 1990; at page 661
245. Sandeep Unnithan, 'When Nehru Spied on Netaji,' India Today, April 20, 2015 at page 31
246. General Alexander Kolesnikov, 'Destiny and Death: Subhash Chandra Bose,' Ezhenedelnaiya Gazeta, January No. 3 1997, Moscow
247. Source: Purabi Roy, cited by Dr Dipak Basu, 'Soviet Union's recognition of the Azad Hind government,' please see link below: http://blogs.ivarta.com/Soviet-Unions-Recognition-Azad-Hind-Government/blog-269.htm
248. From former KGB (FSB) archive. Moscow; Affidavit - Dr Purabi Roy to The Mukherjee Commission
249. Author's Note: I believe that this is a reasonable supposition, one that is also made by Suresh Chandra Basu, Bose's brother in 'The Dissentient Report'
250. Suresh Chandra Basu, 'The Dissentient Report,' page 33
251. Shantanu Guha Ray, 'We are chasing a mirage; Dr Purabi Roy, Mid-day, 4 October, 2015
252. Sagari Chhabra, 'In Search of Freedom,'.
253. Suresh Chandra Basu, 'The Dissentient Report'; at page 34
254. Ibid
255. Ibid

256. Ibid
257. Ibid; at page 5
258. Ibid
259. Ibid
260. Robert J McMahon, 'The Cold War: A Very Short Introduction,' Oxford University Press, 2003.
261. John Lewis Gaddis, 'The Cold War: A New History,' Penguin Books, 2006.
262. Krittivas Mukherjee, 'Indian hero who turned to Britain's enemies was target of failed plot,' *The Irish Times,* August 18, 2005.
263. Subir Bhaumik, 'British attempted to kill Bose,' BBC, 15 August, 2005
264. Anuj Dhar, 'India's greatest cover-up,'
265. Dipanjan Roy Chaudhury, 'Nehru's refusal of Kennedy's offer of nuclear detonation kept India out of the NSG,' *The Economic Times,* 14 June, 2016
266. Maharajakrishna Rasgotra, 'A Life in Diplomacy,' Penguin; 2016
267. 'Netaji files row: Govt forms committee, family hails PM Narinder Modi,' Zee News, 15 April, 2015
268. Ibid
269. Swapan Dasgupta, 'Of Netaji, Nehru and our flights into "history"' The Times of India, 19 April, 2015
270. Ibid; at page 241
271. Ibid; at page 205
272. Rahul Kanwal, 'Who freed India: Gandhi or Bose,' Daily Mail, UK; 26 January, 2016
273. Sagari Chhabra, 'In Search of Freedom,'.
274. Mohua Chatterjee, 'Can't reveal Netaji files, will hit international ties: Govt,' *The Times of India,* 9 January, 2015.
275. Ibid.
276. Sagari Chhabra, 'In Search of Freedom,' page 215.